Tea & C

in the Age of Dr Johnson

The exhibition and publication have been kindly supported by

The G. F. Eyre Charitable Trust
The Rothermere Foundation

Published by Dr Johnson's House Trust
2008

to accompany the exhibition
'Tea & Coffee in the Age of Dr Johnson'
26 September to 13 December 2008
at Dr Johnson's House, 17 Gough Square, London EC4A 3DE

Exhibition curated by Stephanie Pickford and Elizabeth Emerson

Acknowledgments
Dr Johnson's House Trust would like to thank Stephen Twining and staff at Twinings' Shop on
the Strand, Sheila O'Connell, Graeme Clarke, Mary Bingley, Sarah Moulden, Pat Hardy, Peter
Brown, Lars Sonesson, John Fisher and the Trustees, Governors and volunteer staff at
Dr Johnson's House.

Front cover: *Tea (detail)*, Thomas Rowlandson after Samuel Collings, 1786, etching,
Courtesy of the Trustees of Dr Johnson's House

Back cover: ***Lion's Head from Button's Coffee-house***, H. Mutlow, undated, engraving,
© Guildhall Library, City of London

Tea & Coffee

in the Age of Dr Johnson

edited by

Stephanie Pickford

Contents

Introduction

Stephanie Pickford

The coffee-house and the tea-table were two of the most convivial social forums in London during the eighteenth century and were therefore bound to attract the great conversationalist, Samuel Johnson (1709-1784). Of the two drinks associated with these social settings, coffee was the first to take hold of the nation's taste buds and a proliferation of coffee-houses was established in the capital and beyond by the start of the century. Tea took slightly longer to become a national obsession but it soon overtook coffee and the situation remains the same today: as a nation, the British now drink approximately 165 million cups of tea per year and 70 million cups of coffee.[1]

This selection of essays considers the story of tea and coffee in the eighteenth century, when coffee-houses were still popular but had passed their early heyday, and tea fever was beginning to grip the nation. In 1755, when Johnson published his *Dictionary of the English Language*, the British imported four million pounds of tea, and he suggests that double that amount was smuggled into the country.[2] In his *Dictionary,* Johnson defines tea as 'A Chinese plant, of which the infusion has lately been much drunk in Europe' whereas his definition of coffee contains an illustrative quotation from Chambers stating that coffee as a drink has been 'very familiar in Europe for these eighty years'.[3] When coffee was first offered for consumption in Britain, its qualities were questioned: it was called 'boiled soot' and blamed for a variety of different inconveniences ranging from impotence to lack of sleep. However, it wasn't until Johnson's lifetime that tea's reputation was similarly attacked. 'Storm in a Teacup' and 'Tea: A Baleful Influence? An Intemperate Tea-drinker Responds' consider the opinions of some of the major (and indeed less well known) social commentators on the subject of tea.

1. *Tea*, Thomas Rowlandson after Samuel Collings, 1786, etching, Courtesy of the Trustees of Dr Johnson's House

The engraving *Tea* by Thomas Rowlandson, after a drawing by Samuel Collings, was one of a series depicting scenes from Boswell's *Journal of a Tour to the Hebrides with Samuel Johnson LL.D.* (fig. 1). The engraving shows a tableau set in Edinburgh: the long-suffering Mrs Boswell has been told by her husband of Johnson's demand for seemingly endless cups of tea and, forewarned, she attends to his needs appropriately. The yawning servant, low candle and clock showing the early hours, highlight that Johnson is keeping his hosts up late by his excessive tea habit. Mrs Boswell was not the first to come across this: in Devon, Mrs Cumberland served Johnson 12 cups; in Oxford Mrs John Scott used to relate that she had once helped Johnson to 15 cups; Mrs Mudge expressed horror when Johnson presented his cup for an eighteenth serving and poor Lady McLeod remembered that she had dished out a staggering 22 cups to Johnson. On the tea-table in this engraving is a sugar bowl to which Johnson helps himself with a pair of tongs. The British gradually became accustomed to adding both sugar and milk to their tea and the popularity of tea also saw the rise of milk and sugar consumption in Britain. In her essay, Elizabeth Emerson considers the history and effects of this combination.

The tea-table was one of the key social forums of the eighteenth century. Domestic by nature and controlled by the women, it was a place to converse, gossip and also to display one's tea equipage. The nation's love of tea was directly responsible for the growth of Chinese porcelain imports and the explosion of home-grown china manufacturers: Lars Tharp's essay charts the rise of porcelain in this country.

In the coffee-house, politics, commerce, journalism and conversation all thrived; however, in his dictionary definition, Johnson only seems to concentrate on the social and news broadcasting function of this establishment, describing the coffee-house as 'A house of entertainment where coffee is sold, and the guests are supplied with news papers'.[4] Antony Clayton paints a picture of a typical coffee-house during Johnson's time, giving the reader an insight into the costs, clientele, charms and conversation found in these establishments. The illustration on the back cover of this booklet shows the Lion's Head 'postbox', which was affixed to the wall in Button's coffee-house by Joseph Addison and Richard Steele, for the reception of original written work and correspondence as contributions to their widely-read publication, *The Spectator*, thus providing a visual metaphor for the link between journalism and coffee-house culture. Johnson worked as a hack writer for many years and lived in the heart of the printing district of Fleet Street, within walking distance of numerous coffee-houses; he was known to visit coffee-houses with his biographer James Boswell; Markman Ellis looks at the specific coffee-houses that were to be found in the vicinity of Johnson's home in Gough Square.

This series of essays does not attempt to chart the complex history of these two beverages, but instead aims to provide a slice of the story, focussing on Johnson and his contemporaries to provide evidence, amusing and pertinent, of the profound effect these drinks had on the lives of the British.

1   See the United Kingdom Tea Council website (http://www.tea.co.uk/youfaq.php) and the British Coffee Association website (http://www.britishcoffeeassociation.org/page.aspx?page=history&m_id=3)

2   Current experts think that the amount of smuggled tea could in fact have been up to seven and a half million pounds each year.

3   Samuel Johnson, *A Dictionary of the English Language* (London: R. Dodsley *et al*, 1755), definitions for COFFEE and TEA

4   Johnson op.cit., definition for COFFEEHOUSE

Poetry, Science and some Lawyers: Coffee-houses in Fleet Street and Temple Bar

Markman Ellis

In eighteenth-century London, Fleet Street and the Strand were major thoroughfares for all kinds of traffic – on foot, hoof and wheels. The 'chearfulness of Fleet-street', Boswell observed, was 'owing to the constant quick succession of people which we perceive passing through it'.[1] At the centre of this district was Temple Bar, the ceremonial gateway between Court and City. From Johnson's home in Gough Square to the coffee-houses of Temple Bar was a journey of no more than two hundred metres – past shops with overhead signs, alongside paths protected from the constant traffic of coaches and carts by stout posts, and with the constant danger of being splashed by mud or worse as the cartwheels traversed the ruts and kennels of the imperfectly cobbled street. As well as coffee-houses, there were the premises of banks, inns, taverns, barbers, perruquiers, chop houses, brothels, quacks' consulting rooms, spectacle makers, watchmakers, seed-merchants, booksellers, lace-sellers, a tallow chandler, and the splendid spectacle of Maydwell and Windle's cut-glass warehouse.[2] But the area was most famous for its varied establishments for drinking and eating: the satirist Ned Ward described it as 'that tippling street, / Distinguished by the name of Fleet'.[3]

The boundary between the cities of London and Westminster was marked by Temple Bar, a medieval gate in the ancient city walls, rebuilt between 1669 and 1672 to neoclassical designs by Christopher Wren. To the east was the City of London, dominated by commerce; to the west, the city of Westminster, home to the Royal court and the prosperous residential districts of Mayfair. Between the two, centred on the Inns of Court, Fleet Street and the Strand, was the London of learning and the professions. This was the area in which Johnson made his home. The dominant influence on the social life of Fleet Street was the legal culture of the Temple and the other Inns of Court. The inns of court were, and still are, substantial complexes comprising a great hall, library, sets of rooms, and gardens, in which lawyers, judges and their students occupied 'chambers' that served as 'study, office, reception room and place of residence'. Large numbers of established barristers and attorneys also lived in private residences in surrounding streets and alleys.[4] As well as those employed within the legal profession, the area was home to numerous ancillary staff, such as clerks, scriveners, and notaries, as well as trades dependent on legal incomes, such as booksellers and stationers, washerwomen and cleaners, porters and chairmen. Coffee-houses, taverns, ordinaries, and eating houses rounded out the provision for the quotidian needs of the legal clientele.

The most extensive gazetteer of London coffee-houses, compiled by the librarian turned antiquarian Bryant Lillywhite in the 1950s, lists more than 40 distinct coffee-houses operating in the Fleet St-Temple Bar-Strand area in the two decades after 1740: all of these coffee-houses were within a couple of hundred yards of Johnson's house in Gough Square.[5] Some were little known establishments, hardly known beyond the confines of their particular locality. Others were amongst the most famous coffee-houses in London, and as such, significant locations for the intellectual culture of the period. So in addition to the sociability of the law – that of lawyers, judges, clerks – the Temple Bar coffee-houses gave congenial space to the world of learning, most especially science and literature. What all of these disparate activities shared was their love of classical learning and ancient languages, as well as, of course, high levels of education, an exclusive masculine homosociality, and a toleration of the pedant.

In the mid-eighteenth century the pre-eminent coffee-house for men of science was the Grecian in Devereux Court (fig. 2), a winding alley that extended south from the Strand just beyond Temple Bar. The Grecian was named after its founder, a Greek coffee-man named George Constantine, who had come to England as a young sailor; and first opened a coffee-house in Wapping, then later another in Threadneedle Street in 1663, before moving to Devereux Court at some time after 1676. This alley was built on the site of Essex House by Nicholas Barbon, the great Restoration property developer, and was designed as a kind of shopping mall for the Templars, as the students of the Temple were known: narrow enough to keep out wheeled traffic, well lit with oil lamps, and paved with freestone flags. Constantine's 'Grecian' Coffee-House was still being kept by him in 1727, when the antiquarian James Douglas interviewed him for his research on coffee-house history. 'To this Person, the oldest Coffee-Man now alive in *London*, and perhaps *Christendom*' Douglas said, 'I am beholden for several facts here mention'd'.[6] The Grecian continued to trade throughout the eighteenth century, and after it closed in 1834, became a pub, still extant, called the Devereux.

The Grecian, from its proximity to the Middle Temple, was known as a haunt of lawyers, but also attracted men of science. In the eighteenth century, Fellows of the Royal Society – including Sir Isaac Newton, Dr Edmund Halley and Sir Hans Sloane – met together at the Grecian after their weekly

2. *View of the Grecian Coffee-house*, George Shepherd, 1809, watercolour, © Guildhall Library, City of London

meetings of The Royal Society for the Improvement of Natural Knowledge, which had its offices, at this time, in Crane Court, on the north side of Fleet Street, within metres of Johnson's house.[7] Unlike the closed meetings of the Royal Society, both their regular socialising and their club nights at the coffee-houses were open to all kinds of men, including scholars, poets and antiquarians, as well as artisans and scientific instrument-makers. Many commentators felt that the true spirit of scientific enquiry was pursued in the coffee-houses, not in the deadening atmosphere of the committee room. It is in this sense that coffee-houses have come to be known as the penny universities, although the phrase was not used at the time.

Also in Devereux Court, and almost opposite the Grecian, was Tom's

3. *Portrait of Thomas Twining*, attr. William Hogarth, eighteenth-century, oil on canvas, © Twinings

Coffee-house, established by Thomas Twining (fig. 3) in 1706, and in Johnson's time still operated by the Twining family, although they had by then diversified into the wholesale tea trade and banking. But the coffee-house they operated, next to their famous tea shop at the sign of the Golden Lyon, was also a place renowned for its polite and scholarly interests. Amongst the regular customers were two scholars of the first rank in London, both acquaintances of Johnson: Dr Mark Akenside and the Rev Dr Thomas Birch, respectively a physician turned poet and critic, and a clergyman turned historian and scientist. Sir John Hawkins, in his *Life of Samuel Johnson, LL.D.* (1787), commented that Birch was an indefatigable scholar, mining deep seams of antiquarian scholarship amongst the state papers for his various contributions to the history of England in the seventeenth century. But despite this, he was also an attentive clergyman, secretary to the Royal Society, and a man well known to intellectual circles:

> In the midst of all this employment, Dr. Birch was to be seen, at home, at the Royal and Antiquarian societies, at Sion college, at the academy of ancient music, which had long subsisted at the Crown and Anchor in the Strand, at Tom's coffee house in Devereux court; in short, in all places where a clergyman might with propriety appear.[8]

One of the special attributes of Tom's was its library. As well as newspapers and journals, which every coffee-house of any note provided,

Tom's had a large and well organised library of pamphlets and tracts, paid for by a club of gentlemen, kept neatly on shelves for their inspection. These books and pamphlets, comprising all the recent and notable publications, were dominated by poetry, by satires in prose and verse, and literary criticism. At George's Coffee-house, on the corner of Devereux Court and the Strand, there was a similar library. When the poet William Shenstone arrived in London for the very first time on January 10 1741, he lodged in rooms rented from a perfumer, Mr Wintle, above the King's Arms next to Temple Bar in Fleet Street. In a letter to a friend, Richard Graves, Shenstone noted his love for the scandalous and ephemeral poetry of the day, and asked:

> What do you think must be my expence, who love to pry into every thing of this kind? Why, truly, one shilling. My company goes to George's Coffee-house, where, for that small subscription, I read all the pamphlets under a three-shilling dimensions; and indeed, any larger ones would not be fit for coffee-house perusal.[9]

For the coffee-house critics of Johnson's London, coffee-houses were a powerful research tool, providing reading matter, as well as gossip and debate.

Nando's Coffee-house in Fleet Street was located at the corner of Inner Temple Gate, at what is now numbered No. 15. Nando's (the name is perhaps shortened from Ferdinando's) had a long-established trade amongst the lawyers of the district: according to one source, it had a 'lofty bay window at the south end overlooking the Temple precincts', giving those men sitting there a panoramic view of the comings and goings of their colleagues.[10] A satire of the early nineteenth century describes a lawyer following the 'flowery paths of Special Pleading', who, as his 'pocket grows', 'eats, drinks, and falls asleep at Nando's', only to dream of 'mooting' and 'disputing' (a lawyer's rhyme).[11] Nando's had long held literary associations: the bookseller family of Bernard (1675-1736) and Henry (1703-1758) Lintot, publisher and later enemy of Pope, occupied premises next to Nando's, as they advertised on their title-pages. The poet and novelist Richard Graves wrote a flirtatious encomium to a servant girl employed in the house, entitled 'To Molly – at Nando's Coffee House. A Culinary Precept':

> Dear Molly, would'st thou rule the roast,
> First learn to make a butter'd toast.
> Cut it substantial – not too thick,
> Pare off the crust, and toast it quick.
> Slice on your butter – not too thin,
> And melt, ah! gently melt it in.
> Cut it in slices, lay them straight,
> Then serve it in a china plate.
> These rules observ'd, Molly shall boast
> Henceforth to reign – my favourite *Toast*.[12]

The mistress of Nando's, Mrs Humphries, and her daughters, were sufficiently well known to attract the attention of many customers: as one had it, the 'fair daughter was always admired At the Bar, and By the Bar' (a lawyer's joke). Molly, or Polly as she was also known, later formed a public but unmarried relationship with Edward Thurlow (1731-1806), the Lord Chancellor, later Baron Thurlow, living with him in a large house in Dulwich with their three daughters (see fig. 4).

History does not record whether Johnson was a user of the library at Tom's, or found himself amongst the natural philosophers at the Grecian, or admired Molly at Nando's. Indeed, Johnson was not widely known as a coffee-house habitué: Boswell makes little mention of coffee-houses in his *Life of Johnson*. The famous literary clubs that Johnson established, such as the Ivy Lane Club and The Club (later known as the Literary Club), met in taverns. There is some evidence that Johnson – who drank tea liberally – regarded coffee as an extravagant luxury: Boswell records him drinking coffee with Thrale in April 1776 as an 'indulgence' and, on another occasion in October 1779, instructing his servant Frank Barber to 'go and get coffee, and let us breakfast in splendour'.[13]

There is however one coffee-house that Boswell does mention: the Turk's Head. Not much is known about this place, and most of what is known is probably wrong. In his *London Journal*, Boswell associates it

4. *Law and Equity, Or a peep at Nandos*, anonymous, 1787, hand-coloured etching, © British Museum reg. no. 1868, 0808.5645

This satirical print shows Lord Thurlow approaching the bar at Nando's Coffee-house. The bishop following him is saying 'Thou shalt not commit adultery'

LAW and EQUITY, or a peep at NANDO's.

with the Mitre Tavern, located at the corner of Mitre Court and Fleet Street, where he inveigled his way into Johnson's company.[14] The Mitre Tavern was, as Boswell says, 'his place of frequent resort … where he loved to sit up late'.[15] It was at this tavern that Boswell on Saturday 25 June 1763 had his first extended interview with Johnson:

> We had a good supper, and port wine, of which he then sometimes drank a bottle. The orthodox high-church sound of the Mitre, – the figure and manner of the celebrated Samuel Johnson, – the extraordinary power and precision of his conversation, and the pride arising from finding myself admitted as his companion, produced a variety of sensations, and a pleasing elevation of mind beyond what I had ever before experienced.[16]

Johnson continued to dine at the Mitre regularly, often with company, which sometimes included Boswell (for example, on Saturday May 9 1778). Boswell was greatly taken with this habit, which he called 'the custom of the mitre'.[17] Dining, and drinking, at The Mitre Tavern was a habit indulged in by many men of learning and science: Thomas Birch dined there every Thursday with a company of fellow natural philosophers. The great room at the Mitre Tavern was itself a cultural emporium: not only was it the meeting place of the Society of Antiquaries from 1728 to 1753, it was also the location for concerts of music, and for auctions and lectures.

In his *London Journal*, Boswell records that on Friday 22 July 1763, in the evening, a variation was introduced to this custom of the Mitre. On this night, 'Mr. Johnson and I had a room at the Turk's Head Coffee-house, which he encouraged because the mistress of the house is a good civil woman and wants business.   And indeed we found better entertainment here than at the Mitre, and as reasonable. I said that our reason for going to the Mitre was its being an orthodox tavern.'[18] In his diary entry, Boswell associates this coffee-house with the Mitre: and indeed, almost next door to the tavern, at No. 7 Mitre Court, was a coffee-house known as, variously, the Turk's Head (from its sign), or Brown's Coffee-house, or Ned Brown's Coffee-house (from its founder, around 1696), or Joe's Coffee-house, from its then lease-holder, Joseph Witts (from 1742).[19] Such a variety of names was not uncommon in the period: coffee-houses were often variously identified by their owner, location, founder or sign, or even all four at once. Over the next few days, Boswell records further meetings at the Turk's Head: on Thursday 28th and Saturday 30th July, Tuesday 2nd August, and finally on Wednesday 3rd August. He describes their conversation in some detail, and confesses that 'It must be something curious for the people in the Turk's Head Coffee-house to see this great man and poor Me so often together by ourselves. My vanity is much flattered'.[20]

After 1786, when Boswell adapted the material of his London diary, written at the same time as the events described, for the *Life of Johnson*, he recorded that on Thursday 21 July 1763, 'Johnson and I supped in a private room at the Turk's Head coffee-house, in the Strand'.[21] As well as changing the date, Boswell's recollection specifies the place as the Turk's Head Coffee-house on the Strand at the corner of Catherine Street, across the road from Somerset House (some 800 metres away)[22]–although evidence suggests that this coffee-house was not founded until some eight years after the events he was describing, in or around 1771.[23] The name of the Turk's Head, while known also amongst taverns, had been eagerly adopted by coffee-men, including the first, Pasqua Rosee, in the 1650s. Lillywhite estimates that more than 50 distinct coffee-houses used the name in London.[24] While it is not clear which coffee-house Boswell and Johnson went to, it would seem unlikely they would go so far as Catherine Street repeatedly.

Boswell's description of their conversation gives modern readers an important insight into the nature of coffee-house sociability. At their dinner on Thursday 28 July 1763, for example, they talked widely on literary matters, discussing the reputation of writers including Swift, Addison and Derrick, before moving on to Boswell's favourite topic, himself ('we then talked of Me'). Boswell's detailed descriptions of their conversations there and at the Mitre records their interest in literary criticism, literary gossip and moral philosophy. The tone is serious and sober, and despite Boswell's sycophantic obsequiousness, the force of Johnson's sententious and insightful observations is recorded. Boswell's journal, and the account he later gives of it in the biography, nonetheless forms an important record of the conversational qualities of literary criticism in the period, and its integration into the quotidian social life of the coffee-house. Like most of his contemporaries, however, Johnson had low regard for the significance of such coffee-house debates, except for his own. In a letter to Bennet Langton in May 1755 (in Boswell's *Life of Johnson*), Johnson comments that his recently published *Dictionary* 'has yet had no opponents, except the criticks of the coffee-house, whose outcries are soon dispersed into the air, and are thought of no more'.[25] Coffee-house discussions, he opined, were ephemeral, modish, and shallow. Hester Piozzi recorded him advancing a similar disregard for the much celebrated politeness and good manners of the coffee-house:

> To study manners however only in coffee-houses, is more than equally imperfect; the minds of men who acquire no solid learning, and only exist on the daily forage that they pick up by

running about, and snatching what drops from their neighbours as ignorant as themselves, will never ferment into any knowledge valuable or durable; but like the light wines we drink in hot countries, please for the moment, though incapable of keeping.[26]

Addison and Steele in *The Spectator* had proposed the coffee-house as the motor and metaphor for the polite reformation of society. Johnson thought otherwise.

1   James Boswell, *Life of Samuel Johnson, LL.D.* ed. by George Birkbeck Hill, rev. by Lawrence Fitzroy Powell, 6 vols (Oxford: The Clarendon Press, 1934), vol. ii, p.337

2   This account developed from the local topographical survey of Hugh Phillips's *Mid-Georgian London; A Topographical and Social Survey of Central and Western London About 1750* (London: Collins, 1964), pp. 180-88; 281-82

3   Edward Ward, *Hudibras redivivus: or, a burlesque poem on the times. Part the fourth* (London: B. Bragge, 1705), p. 7

4   David Lemmings, *Professors of the Law: Barristers ad English Legal Culture in the Eighteenth Century* (Oxford: Oxford University Press, 2000), pp. 49-52

5   Bryant Lillywhite, *London Coffee Houses: a reference book of coffee houses in the seventeenth, eighteenth and nineteenth centuries* (London: George Allen and Unwin, 1963)

6   James Douglas, *A Supplement to the Description of the Coffee-Tree* (London: Thomas Woodward, 1727), p. 33. See Jonathan Harris, 'The Grecian Coffee House and Political Debate', *London Journal*, 25: 1 (2000), p. 2; Larry Stewart, 'Other centres of calculation, or, where the Royal Society didn't count: commerce, coffee-houses and natural philosophy in early modern London', *British Journal for the History of Science*, 32 (1999), pp. 133-53

7   *The Diary of Ralph Thoresby (1677-1724)*, ed. by Joseph Hunter, 2 vols (London: Henry Colburn and Richard Bentley, 1830), II, June 5 1712 (p. 111), June 12 1712 (p. 117), June 26 1712 (p. 125)

8   John Hawkins, *The Life of Samuel Johnson, LL.D.* (London: printed for J. Buckland *et al*, 1787), p. 207

9   *The Letters of William Shenstone*, ed. by Marjorie Williams (Oxford: Basil Blackwell, 1939), pp. 20-21.

10 John Timbs, interview with Alexander Moncrieff, coffee-man at Nando's (also known as the Rainbow) in the 1780s, here quoted in Edwin Beresford Chancellor, *The Annals of Fleet Street: its traditions & associations* (London: Chapman & Hall, 1912), p. 255

11 John Anstey, *The Pleader's Guide. A didactic poem*, 7th edn (1796; London: T. Cadell, 1815), p. 125

12 Richard Graves, *Euphrosyne: or, amusements on the road of life* (London: printed for J. Dodsley, in Pall-Mall, 1776), pp. 273-74

13 Boswell, *Life of Johnson*, op.cit. vol. iii, p. 24; vol. iii, p. 400

14 James Boswell, *Boswell's London Journal 1762-63*, ed. by Frederick A. Pottle (London: William Heinemann Ltd, 1950)

15 Boswell, *Life of Johnson*, op. cit., vol. i , p. 399

16 Boswell, *Life of Johnson*, op. cit., vol. i , p. 401

17 Boswell, *Life of Johnson*, op.cit., vol. I, p. 399; vol. i, p. 401; vol. iii, p. 341

18 Boswell, *London Journal 1762-63*, op.cit., p. 318

19 Lillywhite op.cit., Nos 195, 865, 1417

20 Boswell, *London Journal 1762-63*, op.cit., pp. 325, 327, 331, 332, 333

21 Boswell, *Life of Johnson*, op.cit., vol. i, p. 445

22 Lillywhite op.cit., No. 1436

23 Advertisements for real estate with a correspondence address of 'The Turk's-head Coffee-house, opposite Catherine-street, Strand' first start to appear in the 1770s: *Morning Post*, June 21 1771; *London Evening Post*, March 23 1773; *Morning Chronicle*, December 21 1775; and *Morning Post*, March 27 1778

24 Lillywhite op.cit., p. 603

25 Boswell, *Life of Johnson*, op.cit., vol. i, p. 288

26 Hester Lynch Piozzi, *Anecdotes of the Late Samuel Johnson, L.L.D. during the Last Twenty Years of His Life*, ed. by Arthur Sherbo (London: Oxford University Press, 1974), p. 148

The Character of the Coffee-house

Antony Clayton

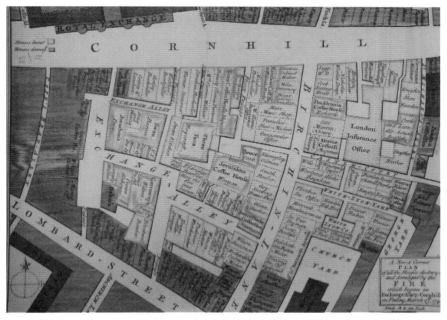

5. A new and Correct Plan of all the Houses Destroyd and Damaged by the FIRE which began in Exchange Alley, Cornhill, on Friday March 25th, 1748, anonymous, 1748, engraving, © Guildhall Library, City of London

It is generally agreed that the first coffee-house to open in London was established in 1652 by Pasqua Rosee, the servant of Daniel Edwards, a Levant merchant who had acquired a taste for coffee in Turkey. Levantines were some of the earliest coffee merchants in Western Europe. As a native of Smyrna in Western Turkey, Rosee had learned how to prepare and brew coffee, a skill that was greatly appreciated by Edwards and his friends, who encouraged and assisted him in opening his own coffee-house in St Michael's Alley, off Cornhill.[1] Little is known of the subsequent history of either Pasqua Rosee or his coffee-house, but the cultural and commercial impact caused by the opening of this small shop in the City of London is still being felt to this day. Within a few years similar establishments were springing up around London to cater for the newly acquired taste for this stimulating drink.

By 1730 one commentator could declare that there were 'a prodigious Number of Coffee-Houses in London'. He went on to note that:

> The Outsides have nothing remarkable or worth describing… most of the Men resort to them to pass away the Time. These Coffee-Houses are the constant Rendezvous for Men of Business, as well as the idle People, so that a Man is sooner ask'd about his Coffee-House than his Lodgings. Besides Coffee there are other Liquors, which People cannot well relish at first. They smoak Tobacco, game and read Papers of Intelligence; here they treat of Matters of State, make Leagues with Foreign Princes, break them again, and transact Affairs of the last Consequence to the Whole World.[2]

During their heyday, London's coffee-houses fulfilled a number of important social and economic roles, including those of postal centres, employment agencies, ticket offices, auction rooms, lost property offices, business addresses, doctors' consulting rooms, gambling dens and masonic lodges. They were places where assignations were arranged, baptisms and marriages celebrated, illnesses diagnosed, criminal acts plotted, votes solicited, feuds ignited, stock traded, scientific discoveries demonstrated, pamphlets circulated and politics debated.

Given the presence of hundreds of these establishments on London's streets in the late seventeenth and early eighteenth centuries, it is hardly surprising that many evolved to cater for distinct social groups and nationalities, or that certain houses began to offer services specific to the interests of their clientele. Scotsmen renewed acquaintance at Forrest's near Charing Cross and in the British in Cockspur Street. Welshmen tended to congregate at Daniel's in Fleet Street, a coffee-house also frequented by heralds from the nearby College of Arms; their presence meant that conversations invariably turned towards, 'births, pedigrees and descents'.[3] Lawyers compared cases and clients at Alice's and the Hell Coffee-house, both close to Westminster Hall. Members of the clergy discussed points of theology at Child's and Truby's, close to St Paul's Churchyard, whilst booksellers conferred on literary and bibliographical matters at the nearby Chapter. Actors gathered at Wright's in Covent Garden; opera singers and dancing masters met at the Orange along the Haymarket and artists at Old Slaughter's in St Martin's Lane. Stockjobbers were discussing business at Garraway's and Jonathan's near the Royal Exchange as merchants were considering the latest shipping news at Lloyd's. Certain coffee-houses around Pall Mall became politically exclusive: Tories tended to gather at the Cocoa Tree and Osinda's, and Whigs at St James's.

What kind of experience would a visitor to a typical London coffee-house have had in the first one hundred years of their existence and what kinds of social activities took place within these popular establishments? Drinking of all kinds was largely a public activity. As easily accessible public spaces, taverns and alehouses were open to anyone who could afford to pay for their drink, and coffee-houses to anyone willing the pay the entrance fee of one penny.

Some coffee-houses opened directly onto the street, or could be found behind other premises that provided access from the street through passageways to rooms at the rear. Many were situated on the first floor above a small business or shop and often consisted of a single room reached by a flight of narrow stairs. On entering this coffee room the visitor would find a bar from which drinks were dispensed; this was often placed in a corner.

Dominating the centre of the room was a long wooden table, where customers sat with their chosen beverage. Scattered across it, a plethora of periodicals, newspapers and pamphlets were freely available to read and study; they might also be found in racks on the walls. Certain thoughtful proprietors also laid out paper, quill pens and ink. Sand or sawdust was strewn across the planks of the floor. The roaring flames in the fireplace not only heated the large pot in which the coffee was brewed but also provided valuable heat in the colder months. The smell of coffee being ground and roasted would have mingled with the odour of unwashed bodies in the already dense atmosphere made smoky by tobacco pipes and flickering candles.

On payment of a penny entrance fee to the person tending the bar, the visitor was free to take advantage of these convivial amenities. Having purchased his coffee the patron would then be invited to take a vacant seat, bench, stool or high-backed chair, where he could drink and chat or quietly read the news material on display. Regular customers often had a favourite seat reserved for them: Alexander Pope, in one of his letters, refers to a 'Speculative Angle', or a chair with a commanding view over the coffee room, which was kept especially for him.[4] The egalitarian nature of this environment is exemplified in an extract from one of the early pamphlets extolling the virtues of the coffee room:

> Now being enter'd there's no needing
> Of complements or gentile breeding,
> For you may seat you any where
> There's no respect of persons there.[5]

As coffee-house culture evolved, the large central table became a less prominent feature of the room. Over time, 'tables were set apart for divers topics', enabling smaller groups to pursue their own interests. A further development, reported by many visitors to eighteenth-century coffee-houses, was the seating of patrons in boxes or booths with high backs, a design that allowed for more privacy. Many of the larger coffee-houses offered the use of private rooms, away from the smoke and babble of the central area, in which business or personal matters might be discussed.

A number of contemporary illustrations provide an insight into the layout, decoration and clientele of the average London coffee-house between 1652 and 1800. The British Museum owns the small, primitive bodycolour drawing which most readily captures the interior and atmosphere of a late seventeenth- or early eighteenth-century London coffee-house (fig. 6).[6] Behind the self-contained bar on the left stands an elegantly attired lady sporting an elongated *coiffure à la Fontange.*[7] She hands one of the serving boys a glass, perhaps of wine, or the Usquebae advertised by a small notice on the wall – no bottles are visible.[8] Coffee

6. *Interior of a London Coffee-house*, anonymous, c.1695-1705, bodycolour, © British Museum reg. no. 1931,0613.2

pots with conical lids are placed beside the fire, over which a large pot containing the boiling coffee concoction is simmering. Handle-less china cups and dishes can be seen around the bar and on the tables. In the central foreground a waiter skilfully pours coffee from the pot with his right hand, whilst balancing the cup in the palm of his left.

A small selection of notices are displayed on the rear wall, where three paintings are hung, one of which is the subject of a discussion between two patrons. Possibly the three paintings form part of a collection that is on display prior to being sold at auction, rather than being permanent decorative fixtures; art auctions certainly took place in coffee-houses. Candles in holders are visible on the tables and on the bar, to the right of the lady dispensing the drinks. Large windows placed fairly high up in the walls provide the majority of the interior light.

A serving boy in uniform is taking a coffee cup from the bar whilst also reaching into a box of long-stemmed pipes placed in front of the bar area; a filled tobacco pipe was usually provided with each cup of coffee.

A relaxed and satisfied looking gentleman is already smoking one of these as he sits at the left-hand corner of the table in the foreground. Another serving boy sits in a chair by the side of the fire and sips from a cup as he waits for his next order. Pamphlets are clearly visible on both long tables and a patron at the right-hand end of the nearest table raises one as if to quote from it, in order to contribute to the discussion. These well-dressed gentlemen sit on long benches, grouped around separate tables, in an atmosphere of calm and contentment, with no signs of argument or inebriation.

Perhaps the most important reason for visiting any coffee-house was the opportunity it provided to pore over the wide variety of newspapers and journals available to anyone able to pay the one-penny admission charge. A foreign visitor in the 1720s reported that, 'all Englishmen are great newsmongers. Workmen habitually begin the day by going to coffee-rooms in order to read the latest news.'[9] It was said that as soon as a customer set foot in a coffee-house, the proprietor greeted him with a request for any fresh news that he might have brought, indicating the voracious contemporary appetite for information, gossip and scandal.

London's first daily newspaper, the *Daily Courant,* began publication on 11 March 1702, although the most widely circulated London paper of the period was the tri-weekly *Post-Man,* with an average circulation in August 1712 of almost four thousand copies. Newspapers from abroad were also available in London. John Macky writing in 1722 remarked that, 'in all the Coffee-houses you have not only the Foreign Prints, but several English ones, with the Foreign Occurrences, besides Papers of Morality and Party Disputes.'[10] By the late 1720s, weeklies like the *London Journal* and the *Craftsman* were selling about 10,000 copies per issue. In 1746 the capital could boast 18 newspapers, including six dailies, six tri-weeklies and six weeklies; by 1790 it had 14 morning papers. Two years previously the first London evening newspaper had been published. The significance of the press was certainly appreciated by Samuel Johnson who commented that, 'The mass of every people must be barbarous where there is no printing, and consequently knowledge is not generally diffused. Knowledge is diffused among our people by the news-papers.'[11]

It has also been claimed that, in the 1730s, each weekly copy of the *Craftsman* would have been read by at least 40 people.[12] Consequently, contemporary opinion on natural science, classical learning, philosophy, religion, art, music and books was freed, in Joseph Addison's opinion, from, 'Closets and Libraries, Schools and Colleges, to dwell in Clubs and Assemblies, at Tea-Tables, and in Coffee-Houses.'[13] *The Gentleman's Magazine*, founded in 1731, contained an eclectic mix of politics, international affairs, science, literature, art and agriculture together with lists of bankruptcies, births, marriages and deaths. It was to provide Johnson with his first form of regular work in London and he wrote the parliamentary debates for the publication for several years. In the first decade of its existence *The Gentleman's Magazine* probably enjoyed a circulation of around 10,000.[14] Accurate and reliable business information was also of great importance during the financial and commercial revolutions of the early eighteenth century. Britain's growth as a colonial power made newspapers and commercial publications such as *Lloyd's List* indispensable sources of information for investors whose economic interests were directly affected by the vicissitudes of war and colonial trade.

Current issues and back numbers of periodicals were available at certain establishments for reference purposes; Peele's coffee-house in Fleet Street was noted for its collection of old newspapers. Some coffee-houses purchased books for customers to read on the premises – they could also be taken home on loan. One of the largest collections of books, newspapers and periodicals was held at the Chapter coffee-house near St Paul's Cathedral.

In a print entitled *The Coffee-house Politicians* of c.1772 (fig. 7), two small groups of men are evidently discussing material contained in various newspapers, one of which is the *London Gazette.* A man seated on the right expresses shock at an item of news being read out from this publication. A curvaceous coffee pot stands on the table in the foreground, close to what seems to be a small milk jug and a bowl of sugar lumps. A coffee dish and a plate sit on the table to the left; various bowls, glasses and jugs are placed on shelves behind the bar. Two fashionably dressed men chat in front of an elaborate mirror that

7. *The Coffee-house Politicians*, anonymous, 1772, engraving, © British Museum reg. no. 1868,0808.13254

The Coffee-house Politicians.

decorates the rear wall – there are no prints, notices or paintings visible. A young serving boy appears to have been distracted by the revelations from the *London Gazette* and spills a pot of coffee from his tray. In the background a woman – perhaps the owner – stands benignly behind the bar whilst displaying an impressive décolletage.

Women were not only employed in the coffee-houses but were also actively involved in running them. It is worth noting that, in the three most widely reproduced illustrations of coffee-house interiors, a woman is serving behind the bar. The social historian Peter Earle has discovered that the running of a coffee-house or some food or drink outlet was amongst the most common of shared occupations in eighteenth century London.[15] However, the coffee-house was generally a venue where no respectable woman would set foot and therefore the clientele base remained mostly male.

Coffee-houses were in competition with inns, taverns and alehouses for the supply of food and drink to Londoners, most of whom, with the exception of the rich, lived in overcrowded lodgings with few cooking facilities. Coffee-houses mostly served light snacks such as sandwiches or biscuits, although a small number offered a more ambitious menu.

Eating houses were popular as sources of tasty food at reasonable prices for the moderately well off. Samuel Johnson visited one when he came to London in the 1730s and Boswell recorded his good fortune: '"I dined", said he, "very well for eightpence, with very good company, at the Pine Apple in New Street [Covent Garden] … It used to cost the rest a shilling for they drank wine; but I had a cut of meat for sixpence, and bread for a penny, and gave the waiter a penny"'.[16] Chop houses and beefsteak houses also catered for the carnivorous appetites of eighteenth-century Londoners. James Boswell described such an establishment in his *London Journal* of 1762-63 as, 'a most excellent place to dine at. You come in there to a warm, comfortable, large room, where a number of people are sitting at a table. You take whatever place you find empty; call for what you like, which you get well and cleverly dressed.' He was impressed that a meal consisting of, 'beef, bread and beer and waiter' (who received a penny) could still be had for a shilling in 1763.[17]

By the middle of the eighteenth century coffee-houses had become an integral part of urban life, supplying many of the essential needs of Londoners and those new to the capital. Johnson confirmed this when he told Boswell about an acquaintance of his who had moved to London claiming that:

thirty pounds a year was enough to enable a man to live there without being contemptible. He allowed ten pounds for clothes and linen. He said a man might live in a garret at eighteen-pence a week; few people would enquire where he lodged; and if they did, it was easy to say, 'Sir, I am to be found at such a place.' By spending three-pence in a coffee-house, he might be for some hours every day in very good company, he might dine for six-pence, breakfast on bread and milk for a penny, and do without supper.[18]

Women could enjoy an al fresco meal and some liquid refreshment at one of London's many pleasure gardens and tea gardens. Vauxhall Gardens was a popular retreat, where Londoners could walk along tree-lined avenues interspersed with arches, statues and cascades. Under the management of Jonathan Tyers from 1728-67, it became especially fashionable as it offered live music and dancing in tastefully decorated supper rooms and pavilions, with a firework display to conclude the evening's entertainment. Plain cold food was available, albeit in meagre portions, together with tea and coffee, wine, beer and cider. A famous depiction of Vauxhall Gardens, published by Thomas Rowlandson in 1784[19], includes caricatures of Dr Johnson, Boswell and Mrs Thrale seated together in a supper box (fig. 8 shows this detail, in an etching after Rowlandson's watercolour). Vauxhall Gardens closed in 1859; unfortunately no trace of it remains today in the busy crowded streets around Vauxhall station.[20]

Similarly, none of the coffee-houses frequented by Boswell, Johnson and their friends have survived into the twenty-first century. Towards the end of the eighteenth century many coffee-houses around the St James's area of the capital evolved into more exclusive gentlemen's clubs, while others developed into hotels. When *Tavern Anecdotes* – a far from comprehensive directory that also included coffee-houses – was published in 1823 the number of traditional establishments was dwindling rapidly. Around the time that coffee was becoming more easily affordable for the working classes, the places in which it had previously been available had in many cases been radically transformed, and new outlets, known as coffee rooms, intended solely for the working classes, were beginning to take their place. The coffee-house was to

8. *Vauxhall Gardens (detail),* Francis Dukes and Robert Pollard after Thomas Rowlandson, 1785, hand-coloured etching and aquatint, © British Museum reg. no. 1880,1113.5484

undergo two more periods of social significance in twentieth century London: in the late 1950s as an integral part of the Soho 'skiffle' scene and, arguably, in the final decade's efflorescence of outlets such as Starbucks, Coffee Republic and their imitators.

1 He also published the earliest printed advertisement for coffee, a handbill entitled *The Vertue of the Coffee Drink, First publiquely made and sold in England by Pasqua Rosee* (London, n.d.)

2 *A Brief and Merry History of Great Britain: containing an Account of the Religions, Customs, Manners, Humours, Characters, Caprice, Contrasts, Foibles, Factions &c. of the People. Written Originally in Arabic by Ali-Mohammed Hagdi… Faithfully rendered into English by Mr Anthony Hilliar* (London: J Roberts *et al.*, 1730), pp. 21-22

3 ibid., p. 23

4 Alexander Pope in a letter to Henry Cromwell 29 August 1709 quoted in Maynard Mack, *Alexander Pope: a Life* (New Haven & London: Yale University Press, 1985), p. 145

5 *The Character of a Coffee House Wherein is contained a Description of the Persons usually frequenting it, with their Discourse and Humor, as also The Admirable Vertues of Coffee By an Eye and Ear Witness* (London, 1665), p. 2

6 *A London Coffee House* (British Museum Dept of Prints and Drawings) is inscribed 'A.S. 1668', a date accepted without question by many commentators. The serving lady's hairstyle and the fact that alcohol is being served prove it to be from a later date, probably c1705 in the reign of Queen Anne (1702-1714). See *British Museum Quarterly* vol. vi 1931-32 pp.43-44. A similar image dated 1730 with several alterations appears as *'A Paris Coffee-house'* in A.M Broadley "The Rariora of the Coffee House" *Country Life* November 1st 1913, pp. 609-612

7 The Fontange fashion in hairstyles was not introduced until 1680, which confirms that the print cannot date from 1668. See R. Turner Wilcox, *The Dictionary of Costume* (London: B. T. Batsford, 1969), p. 140

8 According to the Oxford English Dictionary usquebae or usquebaugh (many forms) meant 'water of life' in Irish and Scottish Gaelic and was an early type of whisky

9 César de Saussure, *A Foreign View of England in the Reigns of George I and George II* translated and edited by Madame van Muyden (London: John Murray, 1902), p. 162

10 John Macky, *A Journey through England . In familiar letters from a gentleman here, to his friend abroad. The second edition, considerably improv'd* (London: J. Hooke, 1722), vol. i, p. 173

11 Quoted in Roy Porter, *English Society in the Eighteenth Century* (London: Penguin, rev.ed.1990), p. 234

12 *The Spectator* ed. with an introduction and notes by D. F. Bond   (Oxford: Clarendon Press, 1965), vol. i, 'Introduction' p. lxxxiii

13 *The Spectator* (No. 10), 12 March 1711

14 See Carl Lennart Carlson *The First Magazine, a history of The Gentleman's Magazine…* (Providence Rhode Island: Brown University Studies, 1938) and Thomas Keymer 'The Gentleman's Magazine' in *The Age of Samuel Johnson 1731-1745* 16 vols. (London: Pickering & Chatto, 1999)

15 Peter Earle, *A City Full of People: Men and Women of London 1650-1750*   (London: Methuen, 1994) p. 122

16 James Boswell, *The Life of Samuel Johnson newly edited with notes by Roger Ingpen* (Bath: George Bayntun, 1925), vol. i, pp. 47-48

17 James Boswell, *Boswell's London Journal 1762-1763*, ed. Frederick A. Pottle (London: William Heinemann Ltd., 1950), p. 86

18 Boswell, *Life* op. cit., vol. i, p. 48

19 *Vauxhall Gardens*, Thomas Rowlandson c. 1784, watercolour pen and ink, V&A museum no. P.13-1967

20 A general account is Warwick Wroth, *The London Pleasure Gardens of the Eighteenth Century* (London: Macmillan, 1896). Though all the walks and buildings of Vauxhall Gardens have long vanished, Roubiliac's impressive statue of Handel, once the centrepiece of the attraction, can still be seen in the V&A.

'The Contagion of China-Fancy': Ceramics in England up to the time of Johnson

Lars Tharp

Derby china is very pretty [but]…the finer pieces are so dear, that perhaps silver vessels of the same capacity may be bought at the same price; and I am not yet so infected with the contagion of china-fancy, as to like anything at that rate which can so easily be broken.[1]

Samuel Johnson to Mrs Thrale, 20 September 1777

Until the seventeenth century 'Ceramics' – the term which denotes the diverse range of all things made of clay[2] – were, in the great majority of English homes, confined almost exclusively to kitchens, sculleries, pantries and cellars: the plain knock-about pots of ordinary households; down-to-earth vessels for the storage, processing and serving of dry and liquid foods (before *and* after consumption). Such 'crockery' was essentially utilitarian, with little if any embellishment. Apart from face-moulded stoneware flagons and anthropomorphic mugs, very few examples of pottery in ordinary English/British dwellings had any association with luxury, still fewer with pretensions to 'art'. If plates or dishes were present at table at all, these were likely to be of pewter or wood (trenchers) or even a simple slab of bread, soaking up the juices and to be consumed once the fare had been scraped off and eaten.

However, in the homes of the wealthy, colourful maiolica chargers imported from Tuscany, or blue and white delft platters (from Holland/Germany or, from the first quarter of the 1600s, from England), might occasionally twinkle from a sideboard, a mantelpiece or from a wall upon which they were suspended – rare splashes of colour in otherwise dark oaken interiors hung with tapestries and with the occasional gleam of polished silver, brass or pewter. 'Porcelain' – until then the rarest of all ceramic materials (though in China already commonplace and manufactured for over one thousand years) was almost entirely limited to palaces and great estates where even the smallest samples were treated as treasures, wrapped in delicate, 'look-at-me' filigree, or 'garnish'd' in gold and guarded in a cabinet of curiosities for occasional fondling. And then came tea …

It is a remarkable fact that, in the 1650s-60s, within the space of a single decade, not one but *three* exotic drinks – tea, coffee and chocolate, each from a separate corner of the globe – all converged on London, eagerly adopted as social lubricants after the social fragmentation of the Civil War. Initially coffee took centre stage, drawing gentlemen together in proliferating public coffee-houses. Also on offer in coffee-houses was tea, a drink extravagantly promoted as having universally curative powers. Both coffee and tea, of course, were non-intoxicating and because they required the boiling of potentially disease-laden water, this meant a lessening of the usual dangers to health. But it was the associated drama of tea-making and tea-taking – the entrance and unlocking of the caddy, the shaking out of the leaf, the pouring on of hot water, the addition of cream, the spooning of sugar, the drinking with extended little finger[3]: it was all this civilized ritual which so appealed to a previously fractured society healing itself after the traumas of civil war, plague and fire. Moreover, it translated well from the public (all-male) to the domestic (male and female) domain. The performance of the tea-table ritual at home perfectly expressed the emerging obsession with 'taste'[4] so that tea, with all its luxury equipage (furniture, silver and porcelain), glided effortlessly into the drawing rooms of the upper and 'middling' classes. For the first time, as recorded in numerous conversation portraits by Highmore, van Aken, Hogarth and others, we see men and women socialising, however briefly, as equals in mixed society. And *the lady of the house presides.*

The taste for tea promotes the acquisition of china; and the infatuation with china promotes the taking of tea.

The Potters' Challenge

Since the 1400s European potters had been mystified: despite numerous experiments, no one had been able to re-create true porcelain/china. What exactly was it? What was the recipe? The fabric (or 'body' as potters call it) was likened to flint, white glass or sea-shells.[5] Most striking of all it was *translucent* and, although light might pass through its white body, the blue patterns with which such wares were usually decorated were somehow intrinsic, locked in or under the glaze. How was this achieved?

In around 1710 potters at Meissen[6] near Dresden in Saxony finally hit on the true (or 'hard-paste') Chinese recipe (for an example of Meissen porcelain see Mrs Thrale's tea-set, fig. 9). It took English experimenters another 35 years to produce their own *soft*-paste versions, around 1745.[7] Meanwhile, the *maladie de porcelaine* – the passion for china or, as Johnson called it, 'the contagion of china-fancy'[8], had taken hold in England. The first victims to what was later to be dubbed 'China Mania' had succumbed after the arrival in 1688 of William and Mary, who

9. *Mrs Thrale's tea service,* Meissen porcelain, c.1755-60,
Courtesy the Trustees of Dr Johnson's House Trust

brought with them to Kensington Palace quantities of Dutch-imported china. This infectious fad spread to courtiers hoping to ape, endorse and align themselves with all the trappings of the new political order. From the early 1700s the East India Company's imports of Chinese ceramics to England began to outstrip the Dutch: from this point on it is estimated that an average of somewhere between 500,000 and 2,000,000 pieces of Chinese porcelain reached England *each year* throughout the eighteenth century. This naturally challenged our indigenous potters. Their response was two-fold: while some decided to attempt china production themselves, others simply adapted their native earthenware traditions (delftware, salt-glazed white stoneware and later creamwares) to create imitations or pastiches of the foreign imports.

In the mid-1740s a number of independent English experimenters succeeded in coming up with their own porcelain formulae. Business partnerships soon emerged leading to the creation of the first English porcelain factories: in London, for example, the Chelsea and Bow factories; elsewhere at Derby and at Worcester. Though most of these failed to hit on the Chinese/Meissen *hard-paste* recipe, some would eventually succeed in turning the relentless tide of Chinese imports. All were heavily dedicated to supplying copious quantities of wares for the serving of tea, coffee and chocolate as well as all the accessories.

Johnson's China

When Johnson sweepingly opines that 'East-Indians' are barbarians, Boswell invites him to except the Chinese on the grounds 'that they have Arts'. To this Johnson witheringly retorts: 'No sir … They have *pottery*'.[9] There's surely more than a hint of tongue-in-cheek: Johnson just couldn't resist another mock-magisterial quip. As we see from the pieces in the exhibition, despite his jibe, Johnson's very own tea wares include several examples of Chinese so-called 'pottery'. His tea bowls are typical of the *famille-rose* enamelled wares arriving in England in the 1740s-60s. Such imported polychrome designs, as well as the plainer 'blue-and white' export wares,[10] provided much of the inspiration for the newly established and emerging English porcelain factories, whose own versions are often so close as to be almost indistinguishable from the originals. We know, from the pieces to have come down to us at the Museum of Worcester Porcelain, that painters on the bench were given access to Chinese pieces, to be copied direct, for example the popular Chinese subject of a 'boy-on-buffalo' was copied by several English

10. *Samuel Johnson's Teapot*, eighteenth-century, earthenware, Courtesy of the Samuel Johnson Birthplace Museum, Lichfield

factories, notably by Worcester in a partially-printed version, c. 1770.

The most distinctive of Dr Johnson's personal tea wares is his English, black earthenware tea pot, decorated in gold with flights of Chinese fancy: figures, birds and extravagant foliage (fig. 10). Made probably in Staffordshire (or perhaps at Jackfield, Shropshire) it echoes those earlier, undecorated red stonewares from Yixing (China), arriving in seventeenth-century London along with the first consignments of tea. But the real inspiration of its gold-on-black colour scheme surely comes from furniture: from so-called 'Japanning'[11] (lacquered wood and *papier mâché*), those tables, chests, panelling, trays and other accessories imported from Japan and China in the seventeenth and early eighteenth century and immediately copied by English cabinet makers up to and including Thomas Chippendale (1718-1779).

In September 1774 Johnson visited Worcester and the Worcester China Warehouse.[12] By then the factory, originally calling itself the 'Tonquin Works' – a direct response to Bow's trade name 'New Canton' – had been active for nearly a quarter of a century. Unlike the Chelsea factory, already dissolved in 1769 to be absorbed by the Derby works (also visited by Johnson),[13] Worcester had survived the transition in taste from Rococo to neo-Classical: thanks to their revolutionary technique of transfer-printing, they were now able to decorate table and ornamental wares with exquisitely detailed designs (from *chinoiserie* to classical ruins), subtle images which far outstripped the hand-painted decoration hitherto done to order in China – and in a fraction of the time.

Printing an image onto paper and transferring it to the ceramic surface was to become one of the most important developments of the English ceramic industry during Johnson's lifetime – and increasingly used by porcelain as well as earthenware manufacturers throughout this and the following century. It also seriously challenged the hitherto brisk Chinese 'armorial' porcelain trade (for an example of which, see Boswell's coffee cup, motto'ed VRAYE FOY, fig. 11) by putting a severe strain on the decorators in China: whereas the complex new English designs, with minute detail and cross-hatched shading effects could be applied in a fraction of the time, Chinese decorators, having to keep up with the new demand for such complex designs, found themselves having to paint increasingly detailed images – right down to the individual lines of cross-hatched shading. When pay is calculated by piecework one can imagine the painter's frustration when having to paint, piece by piece, line by line, every item with something as complex as the 'Fitzhugh' pattern border on the Joshua Reynolds service, (c.1785) when in England this same border design was simply applied by paper in a few seconds.

While English painters might meticulously copy a Chinese or

11. *James Boswell's Coffee-cup painted with Boswell's crest of a hooded falcon and motto 'VRAYE FOY'*, Chinese export porcelain, Qianlong period, circa 1780, Courtesy the Trustees of Dr Johnson's House Trust

Japanese design, we also see other English ceramics (see Johnson's teapot, discussed above) where the painter delights us with a pure piece of pseudo-oriental fantasy – *chinoiserie* – with combinations of figures and animals in scenes or situations in which the Chinese would never have recognised themselves. This ceramic expression of 'Chinese whispers' had already been established over one hundred years before by the delftware (ie tin-glazed *earthenware*) tradition. From the 1730s onwards, new English earthenware technologies emerged – notably salt-glazed white stoneware from Staffordshire and Devon as well as the creamware (cream-coloured earthenware, later to be tinted blue and renamed 'pearlware') in Staffordshire, Yorkshire and beyond; many of these immediately take up and revel in the *chinoiserie* idiom – one of the most appealing and entertaining aspects of England's informal ceramic inventions.

It was out of the creamware tradition, evolved in Johnson's native Staffordshire some time in the early 1740s, that Josiah Wedgwood (1730-1795), England's ceramics colossus, emerged. He transformed English ceramics from a cottage industry to a modern model of mass-production by bringing Enlightenment science to the perfection of clays and kiln technology: adopting the use of transfer-printing technology; actively promoting the expansion of waterway transportation, both of raw materials and finished products; and developing his business through networks and shrewdly targeted marketing techniques. With all these, Wedgwood would lead England and the world's ceramic industry – stoneware, earthenware, porcelain and all – into the Modern era.

The fashion had started with tea and china for the rich. Paradoxically, on the day in 1765 when Josiah Wedgwood presented his *earthenware* service to Queen Charlotte (having meanwhile been honoured with the title 'Potter to the Queen'), porcelain was usurped by a new material associated with Enlightenment, progress and even political reform. Meanwhile, the reduction of punitive taxation on tea allowed both the beverage and the vessels in which it was served to percolate to the masses. From the seventeenth century to the present, tea and china have moved from the erstwhile realm of princes to the works canteen, from mystical luxuries to commonplace commodities.

1   *The Letters of Samuel Johnson*, ed. Bruce Redford, 4 vols (Princeton: Princeton University Press, 1992), vol. iii, p. 70

2   Ceramics can be classified according to three basic clay (='body') groups: *Earthenwares*: pottery fired at the lower end of the temperature range when individual clay particles do not fuse so that the body is porous unless sealed with glaze [group includes terracottas, creamware ('Queen's ware' – Wedgwood's term); pearlware; delftware; faience, maiolica, etc] *Stonewares:* clays fired to higher temperatures where individual grains fuse to form a solid, impervious body not requiring a glaze to render waterproof [group includes salt-glazed grey or brown stonewares, salt-glazed white stoneware] *Porcelain:* also referred to as 'china', a subgroup of stoneware with the extra quality of translucency and whiteness, originally evolved in China whose 'hard-paste' formula (china stone plus china clay) proved elusive to European imitators until Meissen (c1710); 'soft-paste' porcelains are usually identified with French (eg Sèvres) as well as the majority of English factories. **Bone China,** a sub-group of 'hard-paste' porcelain though with 50% added calcified bones, making it very hard, very white and pourable into moulds, developed in England at the end of the eighteenth century and eventually adopted by most English porcelain manufacturers through the nineteenth century.

3   In Chinese etiquette (and perhaps the origin of the English custom?) it is also considered polite to hook one's little finger, known as forming a 'dragon's claw'

4   Nowhere better ridiculed than in Hogarth's painting, '*Taste in High Life*', 1742 where an elderly belle and beau croon over an absurdly minuscule teabowl and saucer.

5   A likely etymology for *porcelana* from which the French and English equivalents are derived, is the name given to a type of cowrie shell, so-called because of its resemblance to a 'little pig'

6   Mrs Thrale's slightly later Meissen tea service is in the collection at Dr Johnson's House, Gough Square, London

7   Germany was first to discover the Chinese 'hard-paste' combination of china clay with pulverized china stone: 1710 marks the official beginning of the Meissen factory just outside Dresden in Saxony

8   *The Letters of Samuel Johnson* op.cit., vol. iii, p. 70

9   In another discussion with Boswell, Johnson expresses a warmer view to that nation when he imagines the admiration and renown a man might acquire by having visited the Great Wall of China

10 *Blue and white* - though not quite a misnomer, this well-established term is slightly misleading: the *design* is painted in blue while in respect of porcelain the 'white' is merely the natural colour of the clay itself; in delftware, however, the white ground onto which the blue is painted is achieved by covering the natural earth-coloured clay in a 'skin' of glaze rendered white by the addition of ashes of tin

11 Although he is speaking of pouring coffee, Alexander Pope refers to both Japanese laquerwork and Chinese ceramics in Canto III of *Rape of the Lock:* 'On shining altars of Japan they raise/ The silver lamp; the fiery spirits blaze,/ From silver spouts the grateful liquors glide,/ While China's earth receives the smoking tide.'

12 Samuel Johnson 'A Journey into North Wales in the Year 1774', Boswell's *Life of Johnson together with Boswell's Journal…*, ed. George Birkbeck Hill, rev. L.F. Powell 6 vols, (Oxford: Clarendon Press, 1934), vol. v p. 457, September 15 1774

13 Boswell op.cit., vol. iii, p. 163 20th September, 1777

Land of Milk and Sugar

Elizabeth Emerson

I therefore pray thee, Renny dear,
That thou wilt give to me
With cream and sugar soften'd well
Another dish of tea.[1]

Samuel Johnson

In this satirical verse addressed to his friend Miss Reynolds, Samuel Johnson describes his habit of taking several cups of tea, sweetened and mixed with milk or cream. This was a practice to which he was all but addicted, in common with much of the rest of the country. Yet tea, and coffee too, had only been known in England for two generations; and their combination with milk and sugar was still more recent. Where did the idea of mixing hot beverages with these products come from? Why did the combinations take such a hold in Britain?

The origins of adding milk to tea are unknown, but the idea but was probably introduced to Britain via China (like tea itself). The use of milk in tea amongst the Chinese was documented in the seventeenth century; as one European writer says in 1685, 'We are indebted to the Chinese for the idea of mixing in some milk, which they sometimes do when offering tea to strangers'.[2] However, milky tea in China was an exception rather than a rule; although known, it was never a widespread custom. Milk itself may be the reason why it was in Europe and particularly in Britain, not the Far East, that this custom came into its own, becoming the norm. It contains between 2% and 8% lactose, or milk sugar. Lactose cannot usually be digested by adult mammals – including humans.[3] The Chinese, in common with most human adults, are largely intolerant to lactose, and thus the widespread use of milk would be inhibited. In northern Europe on the other hand, most adult humans are, unusually, able to digest lactose and can therefore drink milk without ill effects.[4] The habit of drinking milk in tea, once imported as an idea by travellers from China, was able to take a far stronger hold on the northern Europeans than it could in tea's country of origin.

Despite this physical tolerance to milk, however, the English in the seventeenth and early eighteenth century remained suspicious of it. To some degree this was because they were aware that milk could prove indigestible and was not appropriate for everybody.[5] Galen (129-c200), the physician whose theories dominated Western medicine even into the nineteenth century, cautioned against it, writing: 'with regard to milk, it should not be given at all, but only to those who digest it well and perceive no symptom[s]'. Aside from the question of tolerance, Londoners in the 1700s were suspicious as to the freshness and cleanliness of milk for sale, and with good reason. Often sold by milkmaids, who carried their wares from door to door in buckets slung onto yokes, it might be brought in from the countryside – this was appealing in theory but meant the milk was often sour by the time it arrived. Even when fresh, it was frequently adulterated, sometimes with water from 'the cow with the iron tail' (better known as the local water pump), or with worse things.[6] Tobias Smollett, in his novel *The Expedition of Humphrey Clinker*, describes common additions to London milk:

> carried through the streets in open pails, exposed to foul rinsings discharged from doors and windows, spittle, snot and tobacco quids … spattering from coach wheels, dirt and trash chucked into it by roguish boys for the joke's sake … and, finally, the vermin that drops from the rags of the nasty drab that vends this precious mixture, under the respectable denomination of milkmaid.

The demand for genuinely clean, fresh milk in London nevertheless increased as the eighteenth century wore on. Perhaps, as with sugar, the demand for milk grew at this time in part thanks to the contemporaneous growth in demand for tea with which to drink it. Catering to this demand, 'urban cows' – cows kept in the city – increased greatly in number towards the end of the century.[7]

Milkmaids, instead of carrying buckets of milk to customers' homes, might drive a cow or ass through the streets from house to house, milking it as required and thus reassuring the customer of the quality of the goods (see fig.12).[8] Herds of cows were kept in London's green spaces such as St James' Park (most were kept north of the Thames, with milk from Islington in particular reputed to be excellent) where milk straight from the cow could be bought.[9]

The problem of getting fresh milk and cream to put in tea was thus lessened over the course of the eighteenth century, but certain reservations on its use in tea or coffee per se also needed overcoming. In 1680, Madame de Sévigné (1626-1696), wrote to her daughter, 'But why do you find

12. *Certain City Macaronies drinking Asses Milk*, anonymous, 1770, etching, © British Museum reg. no. 1866,1208.874

fault with milk in my coffee? Is it because you dislike milk; for you would otherwise think it the most charming thing in the world.'[10] The fault raised by de Sévigné's daughter was that milk was meant to be good for consumptives, rather than for healthy adults indulging in the luxury of the still-exotic coffee or tea. Considered good for the ill and the young, it was 'a specifick Remedy for the cure of several Distempers'.[11] Tea merchant and coffee-house owner Thomas Garraway in his *An Exact Description of the Growth, Quality and Vertues of the Leaf TEA* of 1660 wrote that tea with milk will strengthen the 'inward parts' and protect against consumption. Samuel Johnson too considered it healthy, once declaring that 'milk was designed for our nutriment; tea [is] adscititious [superfluous]'.[12] However, like tea, which was initially marketed as medicinal, the supposed health-giving qualities of milk did not hold it back from eventual popularity as an addition to coffee or tea. As early as 1685 John Chamberlayn notes that it was used as an addition to both drinks.[13]

The increasing use of milk in tea can be seen from the appearance of bottles specifically for holding milk,[14] and the introduction of the milk- or cream-jug in tea-sets.[15] Johnson's own habitual use of milk or cream in tea can be seen, not only from his verses to Miss Reynolds above, but also in James Boswell's *Life of Samuel Johnson*, where Boswell notes several times that Johnson abstains from milk in his tea as part of his Easter fast:

> On Friday, April 14, being Good-Friday, I repaired to [Johnson] in the morning, according to my usual custom on that day, and breakfasted with him. I observed that he fasted so very strictly, that he did not even taste bread, and took no milk with his tea …[16]

The bitterness of tea and coffee would have encouraged the habit of milk addition too. Milk and cream, being slightly sweet, would balance the bitter drink; they are often described as 'softeners'. However, this problem had a much more efficacious solution: sugar.

Whilst tea and coffee were imported only from the seventeenth century, sugar had been known in England since at least the early twelfth century when it was so expensive as to be initially the preserve of royalty and the highest members of the clergy. It was frequently used medicinally, giving rise to the phrase 'like an apothecary without sugar', meaning anything useless or absurd. Over the years it was prescribed for such disparate complaints as chest pain, fever, disease of the stomach, the Black Plague, and chapped lips, and its value can be seen from doctors' prescriptions which mix sugar with crushed jewels.[17] Sugar prescriptions continued into Johnson's day despite the fact that its downsides were known too: sugar 'rotteth the teeth, making them look blacke, and withal, causeth many time a loathsome stinking-breath',[18] as well as making the unwary eater fat. The English took to sugar particularly readily, as one German traveller in Elizabeth I's England describes:

next came the Queen, in the sixty-fifth year of her age, as we were told, very majestic; … her eyes small, yet black and pleasant; her nose a little hooked; her lips narrow, and her teeth black (a defect the English seem subject to, from their too great use of sugar) …[19]

In 1603, visiting Spaniards noted the same 'great use of sugar', saying '[English ladies] eat nothing but what is sweetened with sugar, drinking it … with their wine and mixing it with their meat'.[20] In the following century the English attraction to sugar remained strong, and spread into the poorer part of the population as soon as prices allowed. British consumption shot from 4.6lbs per capita in 1700 to 16.2lbs by 1770. While other countries, such as France, also imported increasingly large quantities of the product, the British stood out for retaining and consuming, rather than re-exporting, sugar.[21] 'From the rising rate of per capita consumption implied by the retained import statistics,' says historian W D Smith, 'we see that this increased use of sugar must have extended well beyond the elite … into the middle and even lower strata of society.'[22]

13. *The Doctor administering his Gilded Pill* (detail), Charles Williams, 1802, hand-coloured etching, © British Museum reg. no. 1868,0808.7003

Much of this sugar was consumed within that other great British staple: the cup of tea. In its most expensive and sought-after form, sugar consisted of pure white powder, having been refined. More commonly, it was sold in large solid loaves or cones which were sometimes wrapped in paper (see fig. 13). Three sugar cones were often used to advertise

14. *Trade Card of George Farr*, anonymous, eighteenth-century, engraving, © Guildhall Library, City of London. Three sugar cones are shown in a cartouche at the top of the card, underneath a beehive.

tea-merchants, or grocers who sold tea and coffee (see fig.14). These hard blocks of sugar were difficult to break into pieces, and large, curve-bladed sugar-nippers were used to do this. The sugar then had its own bowl at the tea- or coffee-table, from which it was picked up and placed into the teacup with tongs. Some drinkers placed the piece of sugar into their mouths and drank through it. Boswell recounts Johnson's horror at one hostess's lack of sugar-etiquette when making a cup of coffee:

> At Madame ————'s, a literary lady of rank, the footman took the sugar in his fingers, and threw it into my coffee. I was going to put it aside; but hearing it was made on purpose for me, I e'en tasted Tom's fingers.

Tongs, it seems, were essential to sugar, as sugar was essential to both the tea- (and the coffee-) table. Trades in the two products were to develop into the perfect, symbiotic relationship: tea as a vehicle for sugar, each needing the other as its perfect complement. As the tea trade (now far from the first tiny imports of the mid-1600s) swelled to ever-vaster proportions, so the market for sugar grew with it. Johnson himself is a perfect microcosm of the British addiction to tea with sugar. 'He was a lover of tea to an excess hardly credible,' says his biographer Hawkins:

> whenever it appeared, he was almost raving, and by his impatience to be served, his incessant calls for those ingredients which make that liquor palatable [that is, milk and sugar] … he seldom failed to make a fatigue to everyone else, [that] which was intended as a general refreshment.[23]

Many a hostess certainly found this 'excess' fatiguing. One Lady Macleod, having refilled Johnson's teacup sixteen times, finally asked her troublesome guest 'if a small basin would not save him trouble and be more agreeable? – "I wonder, Madam," answered he roughly, "why all the ladies ask me such questions. It is to save yourself trouble Madam, and not me."'[24] On the other hand, when on his tour of the Hebrides with Boswell, Mrs Boswell (doubtless forewarned) made no such fuss over the provision of tea. Johnson thereupon 'showed much complacency upon finding that the mistress of the house was so attentive to his singular habit … his address to her was most courteous and engaging'.[25]

The linked industries of tea and sugar had a darker connection to a third trade: slavery. Britain's West Indian colonies, such as Jamaica, had the perfect climate for growing sugar-cane, but one more ingredient was necessary for the sugar-plantations which covered those islands to succeed: an enormous slave population, imported from Africa. One plantation owner noted that the work which his African slaves did daily would kill a white man. Without them, sugar production could never have reached such vast proportions, could never have been so ubiquitous in England, could never have stimulated the tea-trade in the way it did. Ceaseless work, inhuman treatment, poor hygiene and tropical disease meant a short and wretched life for these workers, and the West Indian slave population needed frequent replenishing with fresh imports. Much sugar profit was therefore ploughed into the slave-trade as planters bought new workers to replace those who had died. Insatiable demand for sugar in England fuelled the plantations, which in its turn fuelled the institution of slavery. British consumers were often aware that the sugar they enjoyed was a product of this human traffic, and many were not comfortable with it; yet they were unwilling to give up their own pleasure, and risk destroying two industries which brought vast profit to the nation. Not until late in the century did abolitionists begin to succeed in forcing the British to come to terms with the misery which this triangle of trade was causing, so far from home. This was a particularly poignant fact for one member of Johnson's household: his servant, Francis Barber (c.1742-1801). Francis had been born a slave in Jamaica and had lived on a sugar-plantation called Orange River. He escaped the dreadful life and early death of a slave when his owner brought him to England and, in 1752 when he was still only about ten years old, gave him into Johnson's care as a servant. Such was the strength of the relationship he forged with his new master that Johnson (always vehemently outspoken against slavery) eventually named Francis as his heir. It was this 'slave-sugar' triangle, which swallowed so many lives like Francis', that paved the way for industrial amounts of sugar to reach England, allowing sugar to reach an ever-growing proportion of the population.[26] No longer the preserve of royalty and aristocracy as it had for so many centuries been, sugar was on its way to becoming truly popular. It is clear that once tea and sugar were available in sufficient quantities, the combination was widely used.[27] Few may have drunk sweet tea with the fervour of Johnson, but between 1700 and 1710:

> the taking of tea and sugar with other foods in the morning and late afternoon had become a central domestic ritual in Britain … the generalization of this ritual … sustained the growing demand for tea and sugar throughout the eighteenth century.[28]

But how did it first come about that the one was introduced into the other, and why did the ritual become so all-embracing? The first question may be the most easily answered, since as with milk, the idea was almost certainly introduced from the East. An account of travels by Alexander de Rhodes in areas such as Hanoi, Vietnam, and Macau, notes:

> This is the way the Chinese take tea; boil the water in a very clean vessel; when well boiled they take it from the fire and put the leaf in. They drink it as hot as they can; if it is cold it is of no use … a little sugar is mixed with the tea to counteract the bitterness …[29]

Several other treatises of similar dates likewise mention the use of sugar with tea amongst the Chinese.[30] Once the idea was imported, sugar entered into its own. Why the habit of taking sugar in tea and in coffee was adopted in Britain with such extraordinary enthusiasm however – enough to affect the economy and ingrain itself into the national character – and the tenacity with which that habit has remained in use until the present day, is perhaps a bigger question.

The fact that tea, coffee and sugar all went through a period of being the exotic product of the fashionable classes naturally suggests that the habit of drinking them together stemmed from the elite, and 'trickled down' to the masses. Whilst this undoubtedly played a part in the phenomenon, fashions change: why did not some other fashionable luxury overtake this one, why did the upper classes not abandon it as it became more popular? What made the habit of daily combining these products different, able to take root so irreversibly in the nation's routine?

Sugar historian Sidney W Mintz suggests that Britain constituted unusually fertile ground for the habit due to the fact that a national predilection for sweet drinks was already in place, thus paving the way for acceptance of sweet tea and coffee. English ales have a sweet flavour, and the traditional alcohols, mead and metheglin (spiced mead), as well as many others, are made from fermented honey. Sweetened wine such as hippocras[31] was also popular. Johnson himself, famously devoted to tea, still enjoyed sweet wine; and when there was none available, would instead drink 'Port, with a lump of sugar in every glass'. A wide variety of beverages, it seems, could be improved with a lump or two of sugar. This trick of sweetening alcohol seems to have been peculiar to the English, since their 'habit of adding sugar to wine was much remarked'.[32] However tea, being non-alcoholic, could be seen as a more self-controlled, more respectable method of ingesting sugar.

This notion of the tea ritual as an element of social 'respectability' may help provide a key as to its longevity and blanket popularity in Britain. 'The consumption of sugar with tea and, to a lesser extent, with coffee became one of a number of significant elements of a cultural pattern that had meaning because it both signified and constituted the respectability of the people who participated in it.'[33] To be hospitable in the proper manner, to give tea or coffee at the proper time and with the proper accoutrements of sugar, milk or cream, tongs, porcelain and so on, conferred upon the giver the status of respectability, a commodity more and more highly valued as the eighteenth century progressed; as opposed to the traditional notion of gentility to which one must be born, one can achieve respectability by demonstrating the correct behaviour.[34] To fail to be both decorous and hospitable with one's tea was a social faux pas. While the behaviour of Lady ———, 'literary lady of rank' who allowed her footman to pick up sugar with his fingers and to blow into the teapot's spout to clear it of tea-leaves was considered notably poor, the right behaviour can improve status. Boswell recounts how one Colonel Stepford, breakfasting apprehensively with the notoriously slovenly Johnson, found 'His tea and rolls and butter, and whole breakfast apparatus … all in such decorum … that Colonel Stepford was quite surprised …'. And while not everybody could afford the best tea, porcelain or white sugar, a tea ritual of some kind was to be found in almost every class and income level. Even the poorest insisted on spending up to 10% of their wretched income on tea and sugar, a habit castigated by many as stubborn stupidity.[35] Why would these commoners insist on buying the luxuries appropriate only for the rich, rather than buying wholesome bread, wonder writers such as Jonas Hanway in his *Essay on Tea* of 1757[36] and the anonymous author of a pamphlet entitled *The Good and Bad Effects of Tea Consider'd* of 1758. They did not stop to consider that a cup of warm, calorie-rich sweet tea was no longer a luxury for Britain's poor, but an essential. Giving quick energy and helping make a poor, cold meal into a hot and more satisfying one, it had become 'the irreducible minimum below which was only starvation.'[37] While the wealthy were still enjoying fine teas drunk from rich silver and porcelain, drunk with pure white sugar, the poor had laid claim to the same products, although served in very different style.

The relationship between the exotic tea, coffee and sugar, added to milk, found in Britain the perfect home. The taste, fashion and economics of the eighteenth century combined to normalize these unexpected unions with unprecedented success, their audience swelling in the course of a century from royalty to aristocracy to the whole nation. They have moved triumphantly beyond the normal and into the essential. Like Johnson, we are no longer capable of functioning without them.

1   *Johnsonian Miscellanies* ed. George Birkbeck Hill, 2 vols (London: Constable & Co, reprint 1976) vol. ii, p. 315. The verses were addressed to Frances Reynolds, Sir Joshua Reynolds' sister

2   Peter Muguet, *Tractatus Novi de Potu Caphe de Chinesium et de Chocolata* (1685)

3   When mammals stop drinking their mothers' milk, levels of lactase, the enzyme which metabolizes lactose, diminish until the animal can no longer digest milk. It is estimated that today, approximately 70% of all adults globally are intolerant to lactose. These 70% are unevenly distributed however. Whilst between 1% and 15% of northern Europeans may be intolerant to milk, it is thought that the figure rises to near 100% amongst peoples such as the Chinese, South-east Asians and American Indians

4   H T Huang, 'Hypolactasia and the Chinese Diet', *Current Anthropology*, vol. 43, no. 5, December 2002, pp. 809-819

5   Some 5-15% of the English are thought to be lactose intolerant today

6   Annette Hope, *Londoners' Larder* (Edinburgh & London: Mainstream Publishing, 2005) pp. 121-122

7   P J Atkins, 'London's Intra-Urban Milk Supply, circa 1790-1914', *Transactions of the Institute of British Geographers*, New Series, vol. ii, no. 3, 1977, pp. 383-399

8   P J Atkins, 'The Retail Milk Trade in London, c1790-1914', *The Economic History Review*, New Series, vol. 33, no. 4, November 1980, pp. 522-537

9   Two elderly ladies continued this practice until 1920 in St James' Park, selling fresh milk at a penny a glass – see Hope op.cit., p 121

10 Marie de Rabutin-Chantal, Marquise de Sévigné, was a celebrated writer of letters, mainly to her daughter Françoise, Madame de Grignan

11 D. de Quelus translated by Richard Brookes, *The Natural History of Chocolate* (London: J. Roberts, 1730)

12 'Anecdotes by George Steevens', *Johnsonian Miscellanies* op.cit., vol. ii, p. 322

13 John Chamberlayn, *The Manner of Making Coffee Tea and Chocolate* (London: 1685)

14 Peter Brown, *In Praise of Hot Liquors* (York: York Civic Trust, 1995), p. 74

15 Gervas Huxley, *Talking of Tea* (London: Thames & Hudson, 1956), p. 57

16 Johnson seems to have been very fond of milk, once telling Boswell, 'I should like to come and have a cottage in your park, toddle about, live mostly on milk…'

17 Sidney W Mintz, *Sweetness and Power - the Place of Sugar in Modern History* (New York: Viking Penguin, 1985), p. 100-101

18 James Hart, *Klinike or the Diet of Diseases* (London: 1633)

19 *Paul Hentzner's Travels in England During the Reign of Queen Elizabeth*, translated by Horace Walpole (London: Edward Jeffrey 1797), p. 34 Hentzner's original publication dated to 1598

20 William Benchley Rye, *England as seen by Foreigners in the days of Elizabeth and James I*, (1865. Sugar in its early days in England was not confined to use after a savoury meal or as a treat. It could be added to foods of all kinds, such as oysters, ox tongue, or vegetables. It might even constitute entire courses served between other savoury dishes, formed into extraordinary models of ships, hedgehogs, flowers, even whole castles or Chinese temples – the ancestors of the elaborate wedding cake

21 Woodruff D Smith and Ralph A Austen, 'Private Tooth Decay as Public Economic Virtue: the Slave-Sugar Triangle, Consumerism and European Industrialization', *Social Science History*, vol. xiv no. 1, Spring 1990, pp. 99-100

22 ibid., p. 98

23 John Hawkins, *The Life of Samuel Johnson, LL.D.* (London: J Buckland *et al*, 1787), p. 354

24 James Northcote *Anecdotes of Dr Johnson*, quoted in *Crokers' Johnsoniana*, (London: 1846), vol. x, p. 3

25 James Boswell, *Journal of a Tour to the Hebrides with Samuel Johnson LL.D.,* ed. Frederick A. Pottle and Charles H. Bennett (London: Heineman, 1936), p. 245

26 In order to extract sugar from sugar cane, the planter, or rather his slaves, would cut the ripe cane and immediately crush it. He would then boil it down in great copper kettles into sugar crystals, and dry it in loaf or cone shaped moulds, during which process the molasses within dripped out, and was used to make rum. Rough brown sugar resulted from this process. If a damp clay tip was added to the sugar mould, the moisture in it would dissolve the sugar's molasses, making it softer and whiter. This latter fetched a higher price in England than the darker, coarser variety

27 It was not until the mid-eighteenth century that it was realised that home-grown sugar-beet could yield sugar; and it was later still before the beet was commonly used to produce sugar

28 Smith & Austen op.cit., p. 103

29 Father Alexander of Rhodes, *Divers voyages et missions en In Chine, et autres Royaumes de l'Orient*, 1653

30 Brown op.cit., p. 50, 54

31 Hippocras, named after the instrument it was strained through – the *manicum Hippocraticum*, or sleeve of Hippocrates - was a used as an after-dinner digestive. It was heavily spiced with such ingredients as cinnamon, ginger, cloves, cardamom, galingale, cassia and many others. It also contained large amounts of sugar: one recipe prescribes a pound of sugar to every gallon of wine

32 Mintz op.cit., p. 135

33 Smith & Austen op.cit., p. 106

34 Woodruff D Smith, 'Complications of the Commonplace: Tea, Sugar and Imperialism', *Journal of Interdisciplinary History*, Autumn 1992, pp. 275-276

35 Mintz op.cit., p. 116

36 Jonas Hanway, *Journal of Eight Day's Journey ..To which is added an Essay on Tea..* (London, 1757)

37 John Burnett, *Plenty and Want: Social History of Food in England from 1815 to the Present Day*, (London, 1966), pp. 37-38

Storm in a Teacup

Stephanie Pickford

In the early eighteenth century, tea was new, exotic, exciting and expensive. Introduced to the British palate in the late 1650s, it wasn't until the turn of the century that the nation fully and wholeheartedly took tea to its bosom, as it was gradually absorbed into domestic and social rituals across the country. Tea's popularity spanned the entire social spectrum and, as with all new and highly fashionable commodities, tea – and its effects on the mind, body, soul and pocket – was championed and vilified. The debate involved illustrious figures, varying from Queens to preachers, and not least of these was Samuel Johnson, a self-confessed tea addict, who went to print to defend his favourite beverage after a particularly savage attack by Jonas Hanway.[1]

The first reference to tea drinking in Britain was in September 1658, when a notice was placed in the *Mercurius Politicus* advertising 'That Excellent, and by all Physitians approved, China Drink' sold at the 'Cophee-house in Sweetings Rents'.[2] The first celebrity endorsement of the 'new' beverage came three years later with the arrival of Catherine of Braganza (1638-1705), the bride of Charles II. On her arrival she is reputed to have immediately asked for a cup of tea, and was probably rather shocked to be presented with a lukewarm glass of ale instead. Catherine soon made tea fashionable in court and high society, leading Edmund Waller (1606-1687), an esteemed poet and wit, to celebrate her first anniversary in the country with an ode to the queen and her favourite beverage:

> Venus her Myrtle, Phœbus has his bays:
> Tea both excels, which she vouchsafes to praise
> The best of Queens, the best of herbs, we owe
> To that bold nation which the way did show
> To the fair region where the sun doth rise
> Whose rich productions we so justly prise

The Muse's friend, tea doth our fancy aid
Repress those vapours which the head invade,
And keep that palace of the soul serene,
Fit on her birthday to salute the Queen.[3]

If tea consumption had been contained within the upper echelons of Britain's highly stratified society, there would have been little cause for eighteenth-century moral and social commentators – including the preacher John Wesley (1703-1791) and philanthropist Jonas Hanway – to polemicise against the drink, and in particular its effects on the poor. This, though, was not to be and tea fever soon gripped the nation.

In the last few decades of the 1600s, however, tea was yet to be consumed in truly epidemic quantities, so perhaps its potentially negative physical and social effects caused less concern. Those trying to promote the new drink wrote rapturously about its positive medical effects. Soon after opening his popular coffee-house on Exchange Alley in 1759, Thomas Garraway published *An Exact Description of the Growth, Quality and Vertues of the Leaf TEA* to inform current and potential customers about the benefits of this new beverage. Garraway created a long list of all the particular virtues of tea, which included vanquishing heavy dreams, improving the memory, making the body 'active and lusty', expelling infection, removing 'obstructions of the spleen', engendering good appetite and digestion (particularly for men of corpulent body) and so the list goes on.[4] Tea was sold in the coffee-houses, but its other major retailer was the apothecary as it was initially considered a medicinal rather than social beverage. Samuel Pepys noted in 1667 that his wife was making tea 'which Mr Pelling the potticary tells her is good for her cold and defluxions'.[5] Physicians began to consider the effects of tea on the body and mind and conducted a range of tests on the beverage.

In one bizarre experiment, James Lacy injected a dog with bohea tea but found this made little change to the unfortunate dog. Lacy noticed, however, that, after bleeding the dog, the blood he had collected had not congealed after three days, and he therefore concluded that tea caused an anti-coagulant effect.[6] Others felt that hot drinks would have the opposite effect: a contributor to *The Gentleman's Magazine* in 1750 warns his readers that 'such very hot liquors … thicken the blood', quoting the experiments of the Dutch physician Dr Boerhaave to back up his claims.[7] He goes on to assert that 'it is the unanimous opinion of physicians, that the principal hurt of tea, &tc lies in drinking them too hot'. In an attempt to demonstrate the potentially harmful effects of hot liquors, a certain Dr Hale placed a suckling pig's tail into hot green tea (reportedly 50 degrees hotter than the blood) for a minute. He observed that this caused the tail to become scalded and the hair came off with ease. Hale then cut off the burnt tip of the poor animal's tail and repeated the experiment with slightly cooler water, although still 30 degrees hotter than the blood. The result was similar, in that the hair came off easily. It was felt that the only conclusion that could be drawn was that if hot water caused this amount of harm to an animal's tail, it must cause extensive damage to the lining of the human stomach.[8]

15. *Portrait of John Wesley*, John Greenwood after Nathanial Hone, 1770, mezzotint, © British Museum reg. no. 1893,0411.23

Perhaps surprisingly for those who now equate the Methodist church with tea drinking and the temperance movement, its founder John Wesley (fig. 15) was ardently anti-tea. He even went so far as to publish a letter to a friend in which he warns of the effects of tea on health and finances. Wesley suggests that tea caused many 'Paralytic Disorders' and reports that he noticed a shaking of his hand that stopped after giving up tea for a day or two. Wesley also asserts that tea caused

unstrung nerves and decaying bodily strength.[9] Jonas Hanway (fig. 16), perhaps tea's greatest antagonist, published his diatribe against tea in the form of a series of letters in 1756, with an expanded and revised version appearing in 1757. Hanway states that our own great physicians mostly agree that tea is pernicious but fails to quote any directly at this point. He does, however, mention the advice of Dr Cheyne who, though in general an advocate of tea, admits some persons of weaker nerves may experience a lowness of spirits if they over-indulge. Hanway takes this to its extreme conclusion suggesting that 'since tea has been in fashion, even suicide has been more familiar than in times past'.[10]

16. *Jonas Hanway Esquire*, Robert Dunkarton after Edward Edwards, 1780, mezzotint, © British Museum, reg. no. 1902,1011.786

Johnson's talented biographer, James Boswell, felt that tea had the opposite effect on his disposition to that proposed by Hanway. In his *London Journal* he states that, despite having a terrible day, things started to look up when he had a cup of tea:

> Well, the human mind is really curious: I can answer for my own. For here now in the space of a few hours I was a dull and a miserable, a clever and a happy mortal, and all without the intervention of any external cause, except a dish of green tea, which indeed is a most kind remedy in cases of this kind. Often

have I found relief from it. I am so fond of tea that I could write a whole dissertation on its virtues. It comforts and enlivens without the risks attendant on spirituous liquors. Gentle herb! Let the florid grape yield to thee.[11]

Boswell never did write a dissertation on tea's virtues, leaving this task instead to his friend and mentor Samuel Johnson.

Drinking tea in the eighteenth century did carry some health risks, not necessarily due to the tea itself, but rather to the adulterous materials that were added to the prized leaf. Adulteration was a common problem and sly money-makers would add substances ranging from leaves of other plants, second hand leaves, sheep dung and copper dyes to increase the weight and to ensure the resultant brew was of a colour that would not to betray its lack of purity. Maids would dry their mistresses' used tea leaves in a solution of Japan earth, thereby 'converting' green tea to the increasingly popular bohea, and sell them on. Laws were soon put in place to try and prevent adulteration but the practice continued. There was also a great variation in tea quality and the poor could only afford the worst sort. Hanway suggests that the British in general were often sold poor quality tea and that the difference between what was sold in Amsterdam or Emden or London was as great as the difference between 'raw cabbage and a pineapple'.[12] Johnson was acutely aware of his inability to afford the higher quality teas during his poverty-stricken early career in London and once exclaimed to his successful friend, the actor David Garrick, 'Davy, I do not envy you your money nor your fine acquaintance, but I envy you your power of drinking such tea as this.'[13]

Most of the anti-tea campaigners in the eighteenth century were not necessarily opposed to the drink itself but rather to its complete adoption by the lower, poorer classes and the subsequent effects on their health, happiness and poverty levels. Once tea had become the drink of the elegant and fashionable, the custom seeped through to the lower classes of British society – as Hanway despairs 'It is the curse of this nation, that the *laborer* and *mechanic* will *ape* the *lord*'.[14] In 1742 a complaint was made that 'the meanest families, even the labouring people in Scotland, made their morning meal of tea to the disuse of ale'.[15] Interestingly, both

17. *The tea-table*, anonymous, 1710, etching and engraving, © British Museum
reg. no. 1868,0808.3445

Wesley and Hanway wrote their concerns against tea in the form of a letter to a friend and both urge the recipients to stop their own tea habit in order that others lower down the social scale may follow their example. Simon Mason, whose broadside *The Good and Bad Effects of Tea Consider'd...* of 1745 had the expressed aim of acting as:

> a Dissuasive against an imprudent use of Tea, by Persons of an inferior Rank, and mean Abilities: As for those of superior Degree and Fortune, they are not so liable to the same Inconvenience, by a Superfluous Use of this fashionable Liquor, but may receive many Advantages from it.[16]

Samuel Johnson also concurred that it was not a suitable beverage for the lower classes stating that tea:

> is a barren superfluity, to which those who can hardly procure what nature requires, cannot prudently habituate themselves. Its proper use is to amuse the idle, and relax the studious, and dilute the full meals of those who cannot use exercise, and will not use abstinence.[17]

Johnson insists that it is not simply tea that inconveniences the poor, but instead a general shift towards luxury and idleness ill-befitting the lifestyle or budget of the labouring classes.

The tea-table was frequently associated with idleness, gossip, scandal and a loosening of tongues. The character of Lady Gentle in Colley Cibber's play *The Lady's Last Stake* accuses tea thus: 'thou innocent Pretence for bringing the Wicked of both Sexes together in a Morning; thou Female Tongue-running ... Cordial'.[18] A satirical broadsheet of 1710 (fig.17) depicts a tea-table scene with six fashionable ladies enjoying their tea, whilst in the distance a personification of Evil, brandishing a snake and fire, chases out personifications of virtue – possibly representing Truth and Justice. The verse underneath includes the lines:

Thick Scandal circulate with right Bohea
There Source of blackning Falsehoods Mint of Lies
Each Dame th'improvment of her Talent tries,
And at each Sip a Lady's Honour Dies.[19]

'Mr Careful', writing to the *Female Spectator* in 1745, declares that the tea-table is a 'Source of Idleness, by engrossing those Hours which ought to be employed in honest endeavour'.[20] The encouragement of gossip and idleness were perhaps the least harmful of all tea's alleged distasteful effects.

Financial considerations were the main reason that philanthropists and moral essayists felt tea was unsuitable for the poor. When Sir Frederick Martin Eden toured Britain in the 1790s, just after Johnson's time, he determined that the poor would spend up to 10% of their income on tea and the necessary additions of milk and sugar.[21] Hanway calculated that a nurse drinking a modest two cups a day would need 14d out of a weekly allowance of 30d to spend on tea and sugar; the conclusion being that less was spent on wholesome foods for her and the infant(s) in her charge. Hanway again takes his argument to the extreme suggesting this is one reason why the 'deluding drug' causes the 'diminution of our numbers'.[22]

Wesley advised that if those suffering from 'Paralytic Disorders' were to give up tea they 'might not only lessen their Pain, but in some degree their Poverty too. For they would be able to work (as well as to save) considerably more than they can do now'.[23] This money could then be used for their own benefit or to help benefit those less fortunate. Wesley calculated that his extended family saved upwards of £50 a year when they gave up tea. At this time, Johnson's rent and bills for his house at Gough Square set him back between £25 to £30 per annum. Wesley's saving was therefore a significant amount. Three years earlier, the aforementioned writer to the *Female Spectator* advised that 'the Tea-Table ... costs more to support than would maintain two Children at Nurse'.[24] Wesley also states he was able to assist more than fifty of the poor with the money he had saved through not drinking tea.

Tea's detractors gave their arguments a fashionably xenophobic slant.

Even as early as 1678, some were unconvinced of the attraction of this foreign import, as Mr Henry Savile demonstrates in his letter to his uncle, Henry Coventry, when he describes tea as 'a base unworthy Indian practice ... The truth is, all nations are grown so wicked as to have some of these filthy customs'.[25] The fact that the drink wasn't British and that native products were being cast aside for foreign fashions was one of the arguments that permeated the eighteenth century. Britain was a nation at war for much of the century and patriotism was strong. Social and moral commentators who campaigned against tea often pointed out the virtues of home-grown produce as a viable and cheap alternative to the Chinese infusion. Both Wesley and Hanway suggest a range of substitutes to tea consumption, including infusions of lavender, wild thyme and 'ground-ivy' (the latter apparently best taken with a bit of lemon juice) and sage, green balm or Pennyroyal tea. Mason declared that 'Sage is better on every account'.[26] Wesley also suggests taking a half pint of warmed milk every morning with a little bread to help wean oneself off the tea habit.

Some critics went further than exhorting the benefits of local produce and took a patriotic stand in their campaign against tea. Hanway declares:

> To what height of folly must a nation be arrived, when the *common people* are not satisfied with the *wholesome food* at *home*, but must go to the remotest regions to please the *vicious palate*.[27]

Going his customary step further, Hanway suggests that tea was emasculating the population, thus diminishing the ability of Britons to fight the enemy:

> He who should be able to drive three Frenchmen before him, or she who might be a breeder of such a race of men, are to be seen sipping their tea.... some of the most effeminate people on the face of the whole earth [the Chinese], whose example we, as a *wise*, *active*, and *warlike* nation, would least desire to imitate, are the greatest *sippers* ...[28]

The tea-table was considered to be the responsibility of the ladies and it was always the female head of the family who presided over the tea kettle and teapot. Johnson's biographers declare that his love for tea was far from masculine, Sir John Hawkins referring to Johnson's 'unmanly' thirst for tea.[29] Although this may seem curious now, effeminacy was a term usually used to mock the arch-enemies, the French, and heaven forbid that the British should turn out like them!

For a nation that has become accustomed to a drink that is cheap and readily available, it is difficult to imagine the joy that Pitt's Commutation Act of 1784 – which effectively reduced the tax on tea from 119% to 12% – must have given to law abiding tea-drinkers. Debates over tea and its effects on health continue to this day, although we would struggle to find a critic as vehement as Hanway or a champion as erudite as Johnson.

1   See Lars Tharp 'Tea: A Baleful Influence? An Intemperate Tea-drinker Responds' pp 61-64 for more on Johnson's arguments

2   *Mercurius Politicus*, 23 September 1658

3   *The Poetical Works of Edmund Waller and Sir John Denham*, ed. George Gilfillan (Edinburgh: James Nichol, 1857), p. 104

4   Thomas Garraway, *An Exact Description of the Growth, Quality and Vertues of the Leaf Tea* (London, c.1660)

5   *Diary of Samuel Pepys*, ed. Robert Latham and William Matthews, (London: G. Bell & Sons, 1970), vol. i, xxiv-v

6   Richard Helsham, *An Essay on the nature, use and abuse of Tea, in a letter to a lady; with an account of its mechanical operation* (London, 1722), pp. 20-1

7   *The Gentleman's Magazine*, vol. xx, May 1750, pp. 208-9

8   Jonas Hanway describes this experiment in his *Journal of Eight Day's Journey ..To which is added an Essay on Tea..* (London, 1757), vol. ii, p. 31

9   John Wesley, *A Letter to a Friend concerning Tea* (London ,1748), as reprinted for Wesley's Chapel, London, undated, pp. 1-2

10 Hanway op.cit., vol. ii, p. 77

11 James Boswell, *Boswell's London Journal 1762-63*, ed., Frederick A. Pottle (London: William Heinemann Ltd., 1950), Sunday 13 February 1763, p. 189

12 Hanway op.cit., p. 46

13 CCF Greville, *The Greville Memoirs*, ed. Henry Reeve, 1st series 3 vols, 2nd series, 3 vols (London: Longmans Green & Co, 1874 and 1885), vol. ii, p. 216

14 Hanway op.cit., p. 272

15 The complaint was made by Duncan Forbes of Culloden, as reported in 'The Drolleries of False Economy: Wines and other Liquors' in *Chambers Edinburgh Journal*, No.418, Saturday January 3, 1852, p. 12

16 Simon Mason, *The Good and Bad Effects of Tea Consider'd etc*, (London: 1745)

17 Samuel Johnson, *Review of a Journal of Eight Days Journey*, Literary Magazine 2, no 13 (1757), sourced online via Jack Lynch (ed) http://andromeda.rutgers.edu/~jlynch/Texts/tea.html

18 Colley Cibber, *The Lady's Last Stake: Or, The Wife's Resentment* (Henry Lintot: London, 1747), Act I, Scene I, p. 20

19 *The Tea-Table* (London: 1710). See copy at the British Museum, reg. no. 18680808.3445

20 *Selections from the Female Spectator by Eliza Hayward*, ed. Patricia Meyer Spacks (Oxford: Oxford University Press, 1999), p. 84

21 Quoted in Roy Moxham, *Tea: Addiction, Exploitation and Empire* (London: Robinson, 2004), p. 44

22 Hanway op.cit., p. 73

23 Wesley op.cit., p. 2

24 *Female Spectator* op.cit., p. 84

25 Letter from Mr Henry Savile to his uncle Secretary Coventry, Paris, August 12, 1768, Qtd. in Stephen H. Twining, *House of Twining, 1706-1956* (London: R. Twining & Co, 1756), pp. 11-12

26 Mason op .cit.

27 Hanway op.cit., p. 272

28 Hanway op.cit., pp. 272-3

29 John Hawkins, *The Life of Samuel Johnson, LL.D.*, (London: J Buckland *et al*, 1787), p. 560

Tea: A Baleful Influence?
An Intemperate Tea-drinker Responds.
Lars Tharp

Though tea and gin have spread their baleful influence over this island, and his majesty's other dominions, yet, you may be well assured, that the governors of the Foundling Hospital will exert their utmost skill and vigilance to prevent the children under their care from being poisoned or enervated by one or the other.[1]

Jonas Hanway

So extravagant were the early claims made for the cures and benefits of tea that it comes as no surprise, one century after its introduction into London (in the 1660s), to read social commentators and doom-mongers moving to the opposite extreme, condemning tea and ranking its pernicious effects alongside – and even beyond – those of gin. In the foregoing extract the author, Jonas Hanway (1712-1786), bolsters his anti-tea broadside by quoting the policies of the newly established Foundling Hospital (of which he was himself to become a governor in 1758).[2] Such a witness proved too much for Samuel Johnson, the most famous moral commentator and self-confessed tea addict of his day. We shall see below how Johnson responded to Hanway's anti-tea tirade of 1757. Meanwhile, it would be interesting to know whether another noted moralist, and one of the Hospital's most celebrated governors, namely William Hogarth (1697-1764), was of the anti-tea party: did he too reckon the dangers of gin alongside those of tea?

In 1751, just five years prior to the publication of Hanway's *A Journal of Eight Days' Journey*, Hogarth had published his instantly famous prints *Gin Lane* and *Beer Street*, condemning the evils of gin while extolling the wholesome (and patriotic) virtues of our native ale. But what did Hogarth – the posturing xenophobe – make of the alleged dangers of another foreign fad, tea?

In his painting, *Children at Play* of c.1730,[3] Hogarth depicts a group of children out of doors; their light-hearted play is framed by a grove hung with shadows of mortality – an urn draped with fading flowers, the fugitive

18. *A Harlot's Progress, Plate II*, William Hogarth, 1732, etching and engraving, © British Museum reg. no. 1868,0822.1519

beat of a drum and, at the heart of the composition, a dashing dog topples a toy tea service from a tiny toy doll's table. This dramatic foil – things *falling* to denote fragility and imminent disaster – is one which Hogarth returns to time and again throughout the rest of his career. Indeed, he uses the iconography of an unsettled table with falling porcelain the following year in the first of his 'modern moral subjects': *A Harlot's Progress*.

Throughout *A Harlot's Progress*, Hogarth weaves ceramics, and particularly those associated with tea-taking, into the whole fabric of his story. Ceramics of various sorts appear in four of the six *Harlot* images. In Scene II, our once innocent, now courtesan, heroine Moll Hackabout is seated at a tea-table with her sugar-daddy lover (fig 18). In order to assist the escape of her younger lover (previously concealed in her patron's bed) she kicks the tea-table and launches its expensive Chinese porcelain – teapot still pouring mid-air – to the ground. This destruction symbolises and anticipates Moll's own downfall. The next image (Scene III) finds Moll now in a dingy garret, having lost her patron and forced to swap quality for quantity clientele. Her bunter pours ale from a crude stoneware tankard into the salvaged, once genteel, Chinese teapot, whilst another sad remnant from happier days – a teabowl – stands on the table (and future coffin-stool) by Moll's bed. Moll is arrested and imprisoned in Scene IV and in the penultimate scene, (Scene V), she is shown dying from a venereal disease and the equally dangerous 'cures' foisted on her by two attendant medics. Another lowly table, a poorer shadow of the luxury tea-table from Scene II, lies supine on the floor, with its own scatter of ceramic wreckage. The fall that was teetering in Scene II is now complete. Throughout this 'progress', Hogarth consciously and meticulously used all the trappings of a luxury tea-table to chart a sad decline into poverty and death: from porcelain we move into the world of coarser ceramics to a final stoneware bottle (marked 'Nants', for brandy), making a final visual full stop in the bottom right-hand corner of Scene VI, *Moll's Funeral.*

Does this fall and its use of the tea-taking scenario in some way imply a parallel critique of tea itself – along the lines implied by Jonas Hanway?

Over a decade after the *Harlot,* Hogarth creates his finest narrative series, *Marriage à la Mode[4]*, another downfall punctuated by ceramic markers. In Scene II the ill-starred couple sit separated by a table laid for tea with silver and fashionable china (fig. 19). On the mantelpiece, Hogarth has placed a jumble of china knick-knackery, some seemingly real, but some utterly fantastical, together creating a 'Chorus of the Absurd' chanting a moral denunciation of the modish luxury with which the couple have surrounded themselves. Their family name, Squanderfield, reflects their frivolous spending habits. In the next scene we see the now ennobled Countess at her *Levée* (Scene III)*,* where, while flirting with her lawyer, effeminate admirers sip coffee, or possibly chocolate, from yet more expensive porcelain and her young black page unpacks the latest hoard of auction trophies - many still with lot labels attached. The association of tea, china and collecting is clear: all is vanity.

Nowhere in all his moral panoramas (*A Harlot's Progress, The Rake's Progress, Marriage à la Mode, The Four Stages of Cruelty, Industry and*

19. *Marriage à la Mode, Plate II: Tête-à-tête*, B. Baron after William Hogarth, 1745, etching and engraving, © British Museum reg. no. 1868,0822.1561

Idleness), however, do we see Hogarth railing against tea itself. His true target is luxury and all its pretensions. Indeed, had it not been for the fashionable ritual of tea-drinking among his early patrons, Hogarth's repertoire of social scenarios would have been deprived of a major opportunity to show men and women in company together. His patrons would equally have missed out on the social swagger such images afforded. They show off the owner's wealth through association with tea and all its equipage: porcelain teapot and teabowls, silver tray, spoons and cream jug, and, not least, the tea canister itself, kept in a lockable chest supervised by the lady of the house. Deprived of their tea-table *mis-en-scène*, early conversation pieces by Hogarth such as the *Assembly at Wanstead Abbey*[5], *The Wollaston Family*[6] and *The Strode Family*[7] would have required some other setting. This alone makes us doubt whether the Foundling Hospital's alleged anti-tea policy would have been wholeheartedly endorsed by Hogarth. He was, after all, a man whose early painting career had drawn on this Anglicized Chinese ritual. (His thoughts on coffee would have been interesting: Hogarth's father was arrested for debt after the failure of his all Latin-speaking coffee-house at St John's Gate, Clerkenwell, bringing the dependant Hogarth family within the confines of the Fleet Prison during Hogarth's formative years.)

Another great eighteenth-century social commentator, Samuel Johnson, was stirred to enter the tea debate and he responded directly to Jonas Hanway's intemperate anti-tea broadside of 1757. Johnson abstained from alcohol for large parts of his life – he found abstention easier to achieve than moderation – and so tea became his tipple and many were amazed at his great thirst for this 'watery luxury'. Johnson reviewed Hanway's *Essay on Tea* in the *Literary Magazine* in 1757 to such effect that James Boswell thought it just to remark that Johnson's 'able defence against Mr. Jonas Hanway should have obtained him a magnificent reward from the East-India Company'.[8] Although Johnson concedes that he is a 'hardened and shameless tea-drinker' with a bias towards the drink, his arguments are balanced and rational unlike Hanway's often dramatic accusations and wild conclusions. Johnson's motive in writing seems to have been partly to defend his favourite beverage and partly to dismiss such frivolous argument. He asserts that after Hanway's introduction to tea, its history and varieties, the author 'proceeds to enumerate the mischiefs of tea, and seems willing to charge upon it every mischief that he can find'.[9]

While admitting that tea may not be directly beneficial to nutrition or health, Johnson argues that it both requires the boiling of otherwise contaminated water and makes a tasteful alternative to strong liquors. He backs this up with personal evidence, stating that he, as a frequent consumer, has never felt any ill effect from the drink. In a second article, a response to Hanway's angry reply to Johnson's first review, Johnson emphasises again that 'I have drank it twenty years without hurt, and therefore believe it not to be poison'.[10] Johnson also dismisses one of Hanway's more extreme criticisms of tea: the alleged 'diminution of female

Samuel Johnson

pulchritude'. Johnson wryly regrets that this is a mirage common to all successive generations:

> That there is less beauty in the present race of females, than in those who entered the world with us, all of us are inclined to think, on whom beauty has ceased to smile; but our fathers and grandfathers made the same complaint before us; and our posterity will still find beauties irresistibly powerful.[11]

While Johnson admits there may be a link between tea and the moral decay of the city, this is not one of cause and effect: he points out, in parallel with

Hogarth's visual observations, that tea is just one of many luxuries consumed by the wealthy, its increased consumption being merely a *symptom* of that decadence:

> This general languor is the effect of general luxury, of general idleness. If it be most to be found among tea-drinkers, the reason is, that tea is one of the stated amusements of the idle and the industrious.[12]

Although Johnson produced a huge amount of written work over his lifetime, he was known to berate himself for lapsing into long periods of idleness, as Boswell reports:

> His general mode of life, during my acquaintance, seemed to be pretty uniform. About twelve o'clock I commonly visited him, and frequently found him in bed, or declaiming over his tea, which he drank very plentifully.[13]

Continuing his critique of Hanway, Johnson argues that a population formerly absorbed by the day-to-day rigours of hunting is today still eating and drinking with the undiminished appetites of hunters and farmers when, in fact, modern life no longer involves the same exertions, leaving society to pass the time with cards, dining and sleeping. Tea-drinking, as one of these diversions, he suggests, is a scapegoat; a symptom, not a cause of the negative impacts of an idle life on one's health.

Johnson suggests that most tea-drinkers do not consume great quantities, that tea functions as a ritual providing a focus for other social activities. He argues that tea 'is commonly an entertainment merely nominal, a pretence for assembling to prattle, for interrupting business, or diversifying idleness' and that in general people are brought together not by the tea but by the tea-table and the forum for social engagement that it provides. Johnson's arguments are not totally one sided: he concedes that plenty of time is wasted at the tea-table. However, he determines that as there is no evidence for a shortage of labouring staff, Hanway's assertion that the nation's industries were suffering as a result of tea consumption had little foundation.

Johnson picks up on Hanway's reference to the Foundling Hospital governors' reputed prohibition of tea, quoted above, suggesting that tea was far less dangerous to the children's future wellbeing than a lack of devotional habits:

> I know not upon what observation Mr Hanway founds his confidence in the governours of the Foundling Hospital, men of whom I have not any knowledge, but whom I entreat to consider a little the minds, as well as the bodies of the children. I am inclined to consider irreligion equally pernicious with gin and tea.

Perhaps it was this sideline swipe at the Foundling Hospital which caused Hanway to respond with such rage to Johnson's review. Following extensive travels as a merchant, Hanway had returned to London, devoting himself with much success to philanthropic causes[14]. Preventing the unnecessary death of disadvantaged children and turning them into useful citizens was one of his passions. Maybe it was Johnson's criticism of the Foundling Hospital, rather than any of his pro-tea propaganda, which triggered Hanway's ire. Johnson conceded (somewhat patronisingly), that Hanway was a 'man whose failings may be justly pardoned for his virtues'. Either way, Hanway's 'declamation against Tea' caused the great lexicographer to unleash his pen in a memorable defence of the drink: Johnson's review, Boswell observes, 'shews how very well a man of genius can write upon the slightest subject, when he writes, as the Italians say, *con amore*'.[15]

Hogarth and Johnson were two of the foremost moral and social commentators of the eighteenth century: it is not surprising that they both entered the lively contemporary debate on tea – in words and in images. Artist and writer have each, appropriately, left us their vessels of conviviality: Hogarth's English delftware punchbowl, decorated with a roaring Chinese dragon, may be seen at today's Foundling Museum, and at Johnson's birthplace in Lichfield we may see the very teapot – also decorated with oriental motifs – from which the great Dr Johnson served tea. While both lampooned the faddish victims of what Johnson called the 'China Contagion', each man was an eloquent ambassador, whether in images or in words, of his own chosen poison and no doubt appreciated its associated crockery.[16]

1 Jonas Hanway, *Journal of Eight Day's Journey ..To which is added an Essay on Tea..* (London, 1757), quoted by Samuel Johnson in his review in the *Literary Magazine* vol. ii no. xiii, 1757, pp161-167

2 Captain Thomas Coram's campaign, commencing with a petition in 1729, finally bore fruit ten years later with the incorporation of The Foundling Hospital, *For the education and maintenance of exposed and deserted children*, moving to a specially created site in Lamb's Conduit Fields by 1745

3 Cardiff Museum, *Children at Play* is paired with *House of Cards*

4 In 1745

5 1728-1731, Philadelphia Museum of Art

6 1730, Permanent loan to City of Leicester Art Gallery

7 1738, Tate Gallery, London

8 James Boswell, *The Journal of a Tour to the Hebrides with Samuel Johnson, LLD*, in *James Boswell's Life of Johnson together with Boswell's Journal of a Tour to the Hebrides and Johnson's Diary of a Journey into North Wales* ed. G.B. Hill, revised L.F. Powell (Oxford: Clarendon Press 1934) vol. V, Saturday 14 August 1773, p. 73

9 Johnson op.cit.

10 Samuel Johnson, 'A reply to a Paper in the Gazetteer of May 26, 1757', *Literary Magazine* vol. ii, no xiv, 1757, p. 254

11 Johnson: *Literary Magazine* vol. ii, no. xiii op.cit.

12 For more on tea and its suitability for the poor, see 'Storm in a Teacup', pp 51 - 54

13 Boswell op.cit. vol. ii, 1770, p. 118

14 For more information on Jonas Hanway see Oxford Dictionary of National Biography online http://www.oxforddnb.com/view/article/12230

15 Boswell op.cit., vol. i, 1756, p. 313

16 For a flavour of the various ceramics in circulation in mid-eighteenth-century London see Lars Tharp *Hogarth's China* (London: Merrell Holberton, 1997)

Notes on Contributors

Antony Clayton is a freelance historian and author. His publications include *The Folklore of London* (2008), *Decadent London* (2006), *London's Coffee Houses: A stimulating story* (2003) and *Subterranean City: Beneath the Streets of London* (2000). He is a regular guide and lecturer on aspects of the history of London.

Markman Ellis is Professor of Eighteenth-Century Studies in the Department of English at Queen Mary, University of London. He is the author of *Eighteenth Century Coffee-house Culture* (2006), *Coffee-house: A Cultural History* (2004), *The History of Gothic Fiction* (2000) and *The Politics of Sensibility* (1996). He is at present working on a study of the social life of critics in Johnson's London.

Elizabeth Emerson is the co-curator of the exhibition *Tea & Coffee in the Age of Dr Johnson* (2008). She studied history of art at the Courtauld Institute whilst also working for the Monmouth Coffee Company, training baristas. She was employed by the Public Catalogue Foundation before becoming Deputy Curator/Education Officer at Dr Johnson's House.

Stephanie Pickford is the Donald Hyde Curator at Dr Johnson's House and co-Curator of the exhibition *Tea and Coffee in the Age of Dr Johnson* (2008). She edited *Behind the Scenes: The Hidden Life of Georgian Theatre 1737-1784* (2007) and frequently lectures on aspects of Johnson and the eighteenth century. She previously worked at the Estorick Collection.

Lars Tharp is a ceramics historian and Director of the Foundling Museum, London. Formerly a director at Sothebys, he is a frequent broadcaster, appearing as an expert on the *Antiques Roadshow* (BBC1) and presenting several arts programmes, including *For What It's Worth and Hidden Treasures,* on Radio 3 and 4. He is chairman of London's Hogarth Group and has guest-curated several innovative exhibitions including *Hogarth's China* (1997).